I0518420

# My Life Single For Eight Hours

## By Joleena Louise Kelley

**ISBN 979-8-9919279-0-1**

*I dedicate my memoir to my loving parents, my caring siblings, my four wonderful children, and my encouraging husband. I love you all forever.*

# Table of Contents

Introduction ...…….….................................................…….. 1

Chapter 1 Ten of us and our pets ............................ 3

Chapter 2 To know me is to know my parents ……….. 5

Chapter 3 Summers with Momma and chores ……… 11

Chapter 4 My obsession with sharks ..................... 15

Chapter 5 My first side Hustle ............................. 17

Chapter 6 My first fall was a Doosie ..................... 19

Chapter 7 Waiting for my egg to hatch ...…………… 21

Chapter 8 Sister talk on the beach …....…............... 23

Chapter 9 My fine education in Gary schools ………. 27

Chapter 10 My first fight ................................... 31

Chapter 11 From the bee stings to the Lion ………… 33

Chapter 12 From sting to string .......................…... 37

Chapter 13 What do you want to be? ........................ 39

Chapter 14 My first encounter with a gang ………… 41

Chapter 15 What are sisters for anyways? ................. 45

My Life Single For Eight Hours

Chapter 16 My confession and a pastry ................. 49

Chapter 17 Moving to the country ............................. 55

Chapter 18 The slumber party ................…............. 61

Chapter 19 More education ................................. 63

Chapter 20 A different kind of school .................…... 65

Chapter 21 From skiing to concerts ...................…... 67

Chapter 22 The high school years .......................... 69

Chapter 23 It was a bad dream ............................. 71

Chapter 24 Going to Vegas ................…................. 75

Chapter 25 Back to reality ...................…............... 79

Chapter 26 I graduate and move .......................... 85

Chapter 27 Learning about England ....................... 87

Chapter 28 My troubles ................……...................... 89

Chapter 29 England My first job as an adult ........... 91

Chapter 30 Making the team .........……...................... 95

Chapter 31 Stories you never hear ....................…... 99

Chapter 32 My Second Side Hustle ..................…..... 101

My Life Single For Eight Hours

Chapter 33 Oxford, I made it ...................................... 105

Chapter 34 The Rembrandt and the sketch .......... 107

Chapter 35 My send off ...................................... 111

Chapter 36 Moving back home ........................... 115

Chapter 37 Give me that map ............................. 117

Chapter 38 Follow your gut instinct ................... 123

Chapter 39 Ride and there goes twenty bucks ........ 129

Chapter 40 The loss .........................................133

Chapter 41 I know where I was during 9-11 ............ 135

Chapter 42 The final quiz ................................... 139

Chapter 43 She called to say she slept with Jesus .... 143

Chapter 44 The Biggest Fall yet ........................ 147

Chapter 45 My dedicated chapter ....................... 149

Chapter 46 Single for eight hours ....................... 151

Chapter 47 Only make the gravy ....................... 159

Chapter 48 There's no getting it out of me ............. 163

Chapter 49 What really happens in a restroom ...... 165

Chapter 50 The big night ...........................…........... 169

Chapter 51 What more could I ask for? ..................... 171

Chapter 52 Surviving with so little knowledge ....... 173

Chapter 53 The glasses .................................…...... 177

Chapter 54 The separation ...…..........................….. 179

Chapter 55 He never let me fall ….......................…... 181

Chapter 56 Its hard to get anything done ….............. 185

Chapter 57 Make it simple .............................…...... 187

Chapter 58 Encouragement and the scrapbook ....... 189

Chapter 59 My final chapter...At the end of the day 191

My Final words to you all ........................................... 193

My Life Single For Eight Hours

# Introduction

I have been writing this story in my mind for years. Perhaps, it finally needed to be told. As a young fourth generation Hungarian girl growing up in the streets of a murderous and crime ridden city from Gary, Indiana, I survived making it to one of the world's finest Universities in Oxford, England with all the odds stacked against me. As I navigated my way through childhood to adulthood, I experienced a spectrum of everything from joy, tragedy, laughter, heartbreak, and triumph. Upon returning to the United States, my journey as a young woman continued as I encountered the twists and turns as well as the joys and disappointments of life. After being at a point of reflection in my life, I felt the need to put it down on paper to share my untold story with you. I reveal my flaws and my openness while laughing at myself at times during my journey. My intriguing life story is combined with many stories to tell in each short chapter I have written for you with all of the elements of unique storytelling. My book reflects learning how to thank the many people who have wronged me, as well as giving the recognition to those who have loved me. Most importantly, I am leaving something with you that you can reflect on your own life with as we end our journey. These are the raw and unfiltered accounts of my life as far back as I can begin to remember. Keep in mind, some of these experiences are told from a child's point of view up to my adult point of view on how I saw things, experienced them, and learned along the way.

To be a young girl growing up as a street kid from Gary, Indiana along Lake Michigan, I must convey to you its unique setting. I lived in a small neighborhood of Gary along the shores and dunes. The beauty of the beaches and sense of community that existed made it an exciting time to explore and learn, even though Gary was one of the highest crime rated cities in the United States. Given that, as a kid I learned how to adapt and became street smart very quickly. Most importantly, I was given the opportunity and the freedom to explore my surroundings. As much as there was crime, there was also a community among friends and neighbors. It was on the shores of Lake Michigan that I began my journey into adolescence learning how to boat, fish, and stay safe in the waters. My eyes saw of the some of the most spectacular sunsets every evening across the glittering waters. I also witnessed some of the most violent storms roll in over the blazing horizon on the calm lake in a matter of moments. One of my fondest memories was late at night as the locals gathered on the beaches, set their nets, and put on waist high rubber jumpers to wade into the water. The smell of the roaring beach bonfires is still seared in my head. Groups both young and old would assemble together, catching Smelt fish along the shores, and crime was extinguished…Not even a thought. It was a regular ritual to gather, bond, and cook fish right on the shores with tables set up for the catch of the evening under the warm moonlight and glowing lanterns. It was on Lake Michigan where I learned how to cut and scale fish and began my love of fishing. One thing said, you could wade or swim in the waters and know that nothing would ever eat you!!! No Sharks!!! My favorite fish of all.

## Chapter 1 Ten of us and our pets

Our family was close even though I had a lot of teenage siblings growing up in Gary, Indiana. I was the youngest girl, and I had four sisters and three brothers with an age span of 14 years between us in all. Some were blondes, and some were brunettes. Some had blue eyes, and some had brown ones. All in all, we were a huge family. I mean there were ten of us living together with one bathroom, a German shepherd dog, and oh yeah, a pet alligator, too. Many times I would bring the local kids to my house to show off our pet alligator that we kept in old bathtub aquarium in the basement. He had a leash and a collar just right for his size. Sometimes we would feed it one of my sister's goldfish. She wasn't too happy about that, as you can imagine. It was just a little alligator, maybe a foot long, but it would hiss and snarl at you as small as he was. Funny we never gave him a real pet name, but he was our pet and just called him Alligator. I guess you could say our house was the "go to" house in the neighborhood with someone always stopping by. With that being said, my middle brother was the most popular one. We had one telephone line always ringing for him. Since he and my oldest brother shared the walkout basement for their living quarters, I found an easy way to let my popular brother know that had another girl on the phone calling just for him. With the kitchen above the basement, I would pound three times on the kitchen floor with my foot to alert him of yet another call. I pounded a lot, let me tell you.

## Chapter 2 To know me is to know my parents

Momma was a proper woman. She always strived to not let us speak slang in the house. She constantly taught us big words and did her best to correct us when we spoke any slang. One of her pet peeve words was the word AIN'T. With her family migrating from Europe, it was standard practice in our household for her to teach us new and educated words. I guess you could say you couldn't be a greenhorn, not in Gary, especially in our household anyways. She grew up in New Jersey right behind the Statue of Liberty. Her life was full of hustle and bustle as she grew up taking the train into New York, which was considered her backyard. Grandpa was a bootlegger and brought illegal alcohol in from Canada during the Prohibition in his delivery truck when he didn't have a legitimate job. When he wasn't bootlegging, he would box. He even boxed at Madison Square Garden once, so I was told. While Grandma worked at a telephone company, you could say she was really the bread winner in the family. Momma always was a beautiful lady just like Grandma both being elegant, stylish, and proper, even as poor as they were. I always said Momma could be Liz Taylor's twin sister. In the summer Momma would do some photo modeling, went to modeling school, and worked at the telephone company with my grandma. One time my momma was asked to hold a phone at a desk and pose. They took her picture and put her on the cover of the telephone book. She was always a poised young lady with Catholic values instilled in her from a young age from Grandma. Momma was the oldest of three and took care of her two younger brothers. There were always plenty of stories about how she would take the bus into New York with them, window shop, or go to the park. I guess you can say that was her playground, but she was always street savvy to the dangers of New York as well. She always dressed very nicely, even on her days off. I don't recall her ever having a pair of sweatpants. She sold real estate for a while. Boy oh boy, she could cook. I can say that from experience. Her Hungarian goulash and stuffed peppers were outstanding. As I got older, she eventually became a full time nurse obtaining her license. Momma loved the theaters and Broadway shows, that's for sure. She gave birth to eight children, yes eight. All of my sisters, four in all, were beautiful with their own uniqueness. My three brothers weren't so shabby either, one being my twin.

When Mom first met Dad, he was enlisted in the Navy and was in New Jersey during a training mission for the military. He was from Illinois, a mid-west boy. His family came from Europe as well, and Grandma and Grandpa were more conservative mid-westerners. My grandparents were honest, hardworking, and very humble. They met at a roller skating rink, and Dad and Mom fell in love. I am not sure who fell in love first, but I think it was Dad. With his charm and persistence in pursuing her, they were married in New Jersey. Wedding photos of both sides of the family were like the clash of the Titans, mid-west boy meets city girl. My father was a deep sea welder for the Navy. His love of water was in his veins. Dad was also an entrepreneur with Mom doing the bookkeeping most of the time. Sometimes he would sell soap, sell vitamins, owned a fruit stand, owned a t-shirt shop, and even owned a souvenir shop in Miami. He made a killing sometimes and had ten mouths to feed. Yes, you could say my father was quite the salesman. How do you think he won Momma over? Dad was always interested in the latest technology out there. Something I picked up from

Dad was learning how to work on cars. As a kid I would watch Dad set a timing belt on a car, change the oil, or change a tire. I was right there handing him a tool. I guess you could say that is where my initial interest of cars came from. My dad had a bit of a daredevil side to him as well. He was a licensed pilot and loved planes. From time to time he would take me up in propeller planes.

The one huge thing that Dad always did was taught me something new. He would take newspaper articles, give them for me to read, and then he quizzed me on them to make sure I read and understood the facts. He also loved to encourage my artwork as a child, often showing it off and bragging to anyone who would listen. It was through my father that my love of art evolved.

As I was saying, Dad had a bit of a daredevil side to him as well. He loved those planes and flew two different ones while growing up. During his training as a pilot, they completed what was called the stall maneuver. Basically the plane engine was stalled in mid-air flight, and he had to get the plane started again. He loved to take my twin brother and me up in his planes. He would put us in the back on milk crates for a seat and put headphones on us to block the loud engine noise. We would buzz through the air while making back and forth stunts. It was a grand time as a kid being the youngest of eight. This one day Dad really wanted to show us what he knew with his planes. With my brother and me on milk crates, he stalled the engine mid-air to complete the stall maneuver which he was trained for. The roar of the engine was suddenly quiet, and we glided peacefully through the air. Except this time, he couldn't get the engine started again like he had many times before during his training.

Over and over, he cranked the engine. By now we were in trouble heading for the ground. Dad still couldn't get it started as he always could, and I remember seeing the panic on his face as he was preparing us for an emergency landing. As my milk crate titled forward staring right at the ground, I was trying to hold the crate from going into the cockpit by bracing my feet on the floor and hanging onto the back of Dad's chair. Dad pushed me back in my seat to safety. At the last minute, Dad got the engine started as he swooped past the end of the runway back up in the air again and circled around...We landed safely afterwards. Dad made us promise to never tell Momma what had happened, and we made a pack to never tell her anything about that day. That was the last time I could remember him bringing us up in the plane with him. I'm not sure why, because I always knew Dad was just being Dad. I'm sure he thought the stunts with us were a bad idea after all. Now I am positive my mom is reading my book right now and having a fit. So I am asking you, Momma, "Please don't be too mad at him."

Punishment in our house was honestly brutal keeping all eight kids in line. Kneeling in the corner on hard rice on a brown paper bag for hours wasn't unusual. If that wasn't the punishment, I would have to pick out which belt or tree switch I wanted to get whipped with. Sometimes I got whipped with my twin brother's latest Hot Wheel tracks from the Christmas before. Most of the time, it was for not cleaning my room. Both Momma and Daddy would be in the room to punish me. Yet, Dad had a softer side to him. He knew when I had done something wrong, but he would send Momma out of the room to punish me. Sometimes when she stepped away for a moment, Dad would let me put a paperback coloring book in the back of my pants before I got a butt paddling so it wouldn't hurt. When he sent Momma out of the room, he would sometimes take his belt out. Then he would tell me that when he smacked the belt on the bed to cry and scream like I was getting a good butt whipping. Momma always thought I was getting my punishment. I guess you could say that Dad kept some things from Momma when it came to us kids.

## Chapter 3 Summers with Momma and chores

With ten of us, you could only imagine what our laundry pile looked like. In the basement we always had a huge mountain of clean clothing to sort through. We were each in charge of getting our own clothes out of the clean pile and bringing them up to our rooms. Finding socks was like striking gold, and finding ones that matched was even more daunting as I climbed on top of the pile. It was like looking for a lost contact lens on a multi-colored floor, and hitting the lottery if you found matching socks. As I mentioned, half of the basement was an apartment for my two oldest brothers. The other half was unfinished, and it was creepy like a dungeon...I dreaded going down there in the laundry area. If I wasn't in the basement area feeding Alligator my sister's goldfish, you would find me sorting through the clothing pile for my wardrobe. I would run up the flight of stairs faster than a jack rabbit, most of the time with my feet only touching three or four steps just waiting for something to grab my ankles. It was that scary as a kid. One hot summer day our washer broke down, and I was so thankful I didn't have to go down there that week. Momma took all the dirty clothes to the laundromat around the corner with her station wagon full to the top. It was a beautiful day, and all I wanted to do was be outside playing. Momma had other ideas for me. The entire day we filled just about every washing machine and dryer in that laundromat. I watched through the window as other kids whizzed by on their bikes and heard their laughter.

There I was stuck in a laundromat for nearly ten hours on a sunny day. She taught me how to run the washer and dryer at the laundromat, and I was now in charge of washing and drying my own clothes back home. I had to go down into that creepy basement to do my own laundry from now on, not just retrieve them. It was like being stuck in haunted house and waiting for something to jump out to get me. I skipped doing some of my own laundry and often helped myself to my next older sister's clean socks and underwear. It was either that or go back down in the basement to get attacked by some sort of dark creature lurking around. I hid my dirty laundry pile in the back part of my closet until Momma discovered them. Of course, she marched me right down into our enchanting basement once again to wash my clothes by myself.

Momma always was a great cook. She had a huge pot that covered all four burners on the stove. I learned how to make her Hungarian goulash and stuffed peppers that were out of this world. Her beef pot roast stews cooked most of the day, and the sifting smells permeated throughout the house. Oooh, Momma's food. Yummy. The fresh baked bread often followed, and our house smelled like a bakery. She even taught my twin brother and me how to make taffy candy. It was a real treat. My brother would be on one end of the dining room with me on the other end. We would stretch the taffy and pull against each other from across the room. We stretched that taffy as far as we could and came back to do it again. It was really so much fun, and I fondly think about it. If we weren't making taffy candy, Momma would have us help her with other projects. Scrubbing carpets was a big thing in our house. If we weren't helping to clean the carpets, we would have to vacuum. Keeping our rooms picked up was the golden rule in her household. If you didn't keep a clean room, then a punishment often followed.

Momma always had a way of decorating with a sense of New York style. She had a real keen eye for it. She would decorate the dining room with a wall of mirrors and new wall paper. Parts of the house were always decorated with glitzy decorations or glorious wallpaper. She liked to change it up from time to time. She taught me how to wallpaper by running the backside of the paper through a pan of wet paste and putting it on the wall. She would show me how to line up each sheet perfectly. I always loved how it looked afterwards, but I dreaded it. I was the wallpaper helper for my momma all right. With the wet side of the paper placed strategically on the bare wall, I was to stand against the wall on a stool and hold the wet paper in place. Trying desperately not drop the wall paper, Momma would have me hold the paper firmly while she backed away to get a look at our work. If she didn't like it, I would have to hold the paper still as a statue while balancing on the stool until she was satisfied it looked perfect. It had to be perfect. With my arms in the air against the wallpaper, I would stand frozen and told to hold still. My arms would often be so tired and sore that I couldn't reach for anything as simple as a small cup or plate in the cabinet the next day. Yes, I became Momma's one and only wallpaper girl. Every time she wanted to redecorate the house, I thought it was worst punishment than kneeling in hard rice in the corner.

My Life Single For Eight Hours

## Chapter 4 My obsession with sharks

Moving us out to the beaches of Gary seemed like a logical place to move as Dad loved the water. Naturally, we all shared the same love of the sand and dunes with him. I was afraid there were sharks, but he explained that sharks don't live in Lake Michigan. Somehow I began to be intrigued by why sharks couldn't be in the lake, but could in the ocean... And thus, my obsession with sharks began.

My dad and I bonded with newspaper articles, and it began as far back as I can remember. Sifting through newspapers or magazines, we would find the perfect article to talk about long before I could read them. He would explain the article to me and educate me on what it was about with a quiz that followed. We would be at the dining room table, and I would sit in my chair with Dad over my shoulder pointing out certain things in the article. As I vividly remember it like it was yesterday, we were flipping through this magazine. I was so young that my feet dangled high above the ground as I sat in the dining room chair. In this magazine there was a photo of a sculpture with a lifelike shark diving head first in the roof of a real house. What was intriguing to me was the fact that it was a vibrant colored photograph of this massive shark in the roof with its tail peaked high in the sky, but it had no article to read. Just a photo. I remember every detail, and my father seemed just as intrigued at the photograph we had found.

Then he said something I will never forget that day...... He said, "Someday we will go see that art sculpture, and we will see that shark in the roof together. I promise." I never knew where it was located or how we would ever find it, but Dad always kept his promises. And so Dad made that promise to me, and I often spoke about that sculpture to my momma throughout the years growing up. You could say I was obsessed with the fact that Dad and I would see that massive shark together one day.

## Chapter 5 My First Side Hustle

Before I began school, my life on the shores of Gary, Indiana was all I knew to this point. It was a smaller community away from downtown, but I could still walk down to the beach just a few houses away or to my friend's house without too much worry. My favorite thing was going to the local grocery store three houses down to put my penny in the machine for a piece of bubblegum. That is how my first side hustle began. I would sell acorns for a penny so people could feed their squirrels, and I could buy bubblegum. Momma was my first customer. She somehow paid me with a red bingo chip in the mix of her pennies. I guess I got a little tired of trying to collect the acorns and had no way to carry all of them very well. Using an old bicycle seat upside down wasn't working out at all, so I had to come up with something else. I remember walking though the dunes along the shore one day. I found this really cool leather carrier that washed up on shore. It had a waist strap, and it worked perfectly for my needs. I decided I would fill it up and go door to door selling acorns to the neighbors for the great deal of one penny each. My pitch was selling the acorns so people could feed their squirrels and watch them munch away.

Off I went. I made 17 cents that afternoon, but couldn't understand why everyone was staring at my holster so strangely when I reached in to get out the acorns.

I approached this one little old lady's house. She politely gave me ten pennies, and then she swiftly sent me directly back home to my mother. I had the holster strapped to my waist, and of course asked her why she insisted I go home immediately. Apparently, what I had was a gun holster filled with acorns loaded and ready to sell. I never knew what a gun holster was, and there I was carrying one around the neighborhood with acorns! So my side hustle was over before I got home that afternoon, and I ditched the holster before anyone knew. I was allowed to go to the grocery store a short distance from our house, so I made a stop there on the way home. As the pennies from my side hustle began to run out from buying tons of bubblegum, I accidentally put Momma's red bingo chip among my pennies in the bubblegum machine. I couldn't get it out. I had no choice but to turn the knob with the bingo chip still stuck in the coin slot. I slowly turned the handle of the bubblegum machine. Just like magic it worked, and a bubblegum fell right out. Free gum! After that I got into Momma's stash of bingo chips, and then I could get my bubblegum free whenever I wanted to without trying to sell acorns.

I couldn't tell you what ever happened to my first gun holster after I ditched it, but I didn't care anymore because I was getting free bubblegum. It wasn't long before the store manager caught me though later that fall..."It's you!" he exclaimed. Ultimately, he confiscated all of Momma's bingo chips and marched me out of the store.

## Chapter 6 My first fall was a Doosie

Momma trusted my siblings to a watch the younger ones if she had to work, and for the most part they did. This one particular day, my older sister who was seven years older took me with her to a neighbor's along the shore. I was allowed to ride the neighbor's tricycle as she watched. I was only to go one or two houses along the driveways and was to turn around and return. As she watched me, she began to call out to return and come back. I made a sharp turn with the tricycle to return. Being that age, unfortunately the tricycle was way too small for me. My knees always hit the handlebars when I peddled it. I must have looked like a clown in the circus riding it. Anyways, when I was making the sharp turn to come back two houses down, my knee got caught under the handlebar as the bike tipped over. Now in the dunes, some of the houses have a garage and driveway underneath the house. This particular house two doors down had a basement garage with a long and steep slope to the bottom. As I felt the tricycle tipping over, I couldn't stop it and was tangled under the handlebar. My sister saw what was happening and quickly came running to my rescue. I disappeared down the steep embankment of the basement garage.

The next thing I remember was being pulled out and being on fire. The neighbor had started a barbecue pit filled with hot charcoal at the bottom of the slope, and I rolled right into it.

My sister quickly did what she could as she drug me onto the grass lawn. Someone got a hose to spray me down. I remember spinning around so they could hose down all sides of me. I was stripped naked from the burning clothing in front of everyone. As I cried, I remember just feeling embarrassed that people saw me naked more than I was thinking about the pain. It really was no one's fault, and my sister was doing exactly what she was told to do by watching me. It was just a freak accident. Soon Momma and Daddy took me off to the hospital. The back middle part of my neck and the center of my shoulder blades were burned badly. They triaged me and later sent me home from the hospital wrapped in gauze and ointments, as I recall. Every time Momma went to change my dressings, the gauze would re-open my wounds and was infused to my skin. Momma and Daddy had sold aloe vera in one of their business ventures, so we had plenty still at home. Momma and Daddy would soak me in warm aloe vera baths for hours over and over until they eventually healed my wounds. They really believed in the stuff they were selling. It's very strange, but because of my parent's passionate entrepreneurial spirit, I can say that I have almost no scars. It's actually shaped like the state of Illinois. Unless you are looking for it in a certain light, you can't see it at all. So my nearly invisible scar was a result of my sister's fast actions and my parent's aloe vera baths. Actually until I started writing this book, I hadn't brought it up for years.

My Life Single For Eight Hours

## Chapter 7 Waiting for my egg to hatch

As a young as I was, my parents were liberal with us, except for one thing. There was never any talk about sex or anything like that. Never. My mom was proper. Do I need to say more? Pretty much I relied on my older sisters to find out anything. But if you are very young and don't know anything, how do you know what to ask, right? So here is how Mom's big talk went, the only talk ever.

As I explained, we had a local grocery store a few houses down, and Momma would often send me off for bread or coffee. Then this one day I went to the store with Momma and my sister that was 4 years older than me. I always enjoyed anytime I could go into the store and venture a little bit, of course with Momma trying to find out where I wandered off to again. I ended up finding my momma and my sister again in this particular part of the store I had never been before. The shelves were lined up with boxes with of some sort of pads. As Momma was having a quiet and secretive talk with my sister, I felt a little left out. I didn't recognize any of the usual grocery items. Being me, I grabbed this odd shaped bottle full of water with a stem at the top from the shelf and started squeezing it, curious as to what it was. My mother took it from me right away. I asked her, "Momma, what is this?" This is what she said verbatim: "One day you will become a woman, like your sister here. When you go to the bathroom, you might bleed a little bit. Don't be scared. You will release an egg with a little blood, and that's when you will become a woman." She took my hand and purchased the items for my sister, and we left the store.

I was really confused at her explanation. Release an egg? All I remember was walking out of that store and hoping one day I would become a woman, too. That was a big deal to me, and then I wouldn't be treated like a little kid anymore. For the next 5 years, I imagined going to the bathroom and releasing my big ostrich egg to become a woman. Every time I went pee, I would look down into the bowl and look for this big egg I was supposed to hatch. I remember what she said, "Don't be scared." Of course I was scared! I kept repeating her words to myself as I said quietly out loud and looking down, "This is going to really hurt! It is going to be a huge egg!" Thanks, Mom.

## Chapter 8 Sister talk on the beach

You could say I grew up in the watchful eyes of my teenage sisters. They taught me a lot of stuff I guess I couldn't find out from my parents. You could always find me running up and down the beaches with all the locals. As a kid, I had a lot of freedom on the sandy beach. Parents, siblings, and neighbors were always close by, in which as a kid, I was always in check. It was not unusual to find a group of us always stopping by to visit other groups on our walks through the sand. Most would offer you a cold water or sandwich. I never went hungry on the beach, that's for sure. My girlfriend and I were doing our usual socializing and decided to take a stroll further down to another towel and group. We were stopped by two teenage boys along the way. Being so young, we were both surprised and puzzled that these young teenage boys were interested in talking with us. Trying to be funny one asked giggling, "Are you a virgin?" I scratched the side of my face, not understanding the question or what that word meant. I turned to my friend just as naive as she replied, "No (....... a long pause). I am a Leo. So what's your sign?" I followed suit as I added, "And I am a Capricorn." These boys fell to the ground in laughter as I have never seen before. They could not utter another word curled up in the fetal position carrying on in laughter. I mean the gull! They didn't even tell us what their sign was, so we walked away in frustration.

Pounding our feet in the sand, I found one of my teenage sisters on the beach and told her what happened. She too died laughing at us. Finally, I asked, "What is so funny?"

So in her own way, she began to explain what a virgin was to me. In her analytical version of what it meant, she took her right hand making a circle like a hole. Then she put her other pointed finger in the hole with a back and forth motion in a theatrical version of what happens to you. Horrifically disgusted and in shock, it definitely was not a horoscope sign, so I learned.

Along the sandy beaches, I would always find treasure like rocks and unique driftwood. I became a pretty good rock skipper across the waters and would always find perfectly smooth stones to skip with. Most of the time local kids would stay in tight groups and just hang together. Adults and locals always watched out for one another perched with their towels and umbrellas along the shoreline. Naturally on any beautiful, sunny, and hot summer day, most of us played in the water and sultry sands for hours at a time. One day while walking along the beach looking for rocks, I found a closed package of balloons. Pretty cool thing to fill with sand or blow up. That hot summer day, I grabbed up one of my friends to show her the balloons that I had found in the package. Then we came up with the glorious idea of filling the balloon with sand, tying the end, and tossing it back and forth in waist deep water along the shoreline together. The balloons were of an odd and long shape, like the kind a clown uses to blow up and twist to make animals at the carnivals. You know the kind. Anyways, we would go "deep sea diving" as the sand filled balloon would sink to the bottom of the water. The balloon was also see-through and totally transparent, which made it extra special. Even harder to really find at the bottom of the lake. With its transparency, my sand filled balloon became a chameleon transforming to the same color as the bottom of the water. After diving for this heavy sand filled balloon, we decided to start tossing it back and forth in the air, slinging it as far as it would go. Then if you didn't catch it in mid-air, you had to dive for it. What a blast we were having. All of our fun in the blazing sun was suddenly interrupted. People were screaming and pulling their kids out of the water. The parents and children looked terrified. What in the world was going on? I knew it couldn't be a shark, because sharks don't live in Lake Michigan. Did someone drown? The people rushed out of the water so fast that I thought they took half of the lake with them, like a big suction. Before I knew it, my friend and I were the only ones left in the water. All the screaming on the shore got the attention of my older teenage sister who came running down from the dunes. She began screaming at me and running towards us just as we made our last toss in the air..........."What are you two doing!!!!!!!!??????????" She grabbed my friend and me and said, "Leave it." Not my balloon! As my sister drug us out of the water, we were scolded for being responsible for the panic on the beach. I thought, "How could that be? We were just playing." I was looking around as parents were trying to console their children and wrap them in warm towels. My sister took me aside scolding me that if I ever did that again, she would beat my little you know what. She took my package of balloons away. I argued that I had done nothing wrong...Then the reality hit me as my teenage sister explained...My sand filled balloon was actually a condom, and we were tossing it back and forth in the air right in front of everyone on the beach.

We created a panic as ludicrous teenage boys repeatedly shouted, "Danger, danger in the in the water! Get out!" It was all I heard from the shore as we were laughed at by these boys. OK, so my sister then gave me a very brief and short explanation of what a condom was, and what it was used for. Who knew?

## Chapter 9 My fine education in Gary schools

Before I get into my fine education, I have to tell you I was always a learner on my own, a little sponge. I found my daddy's records and some books. They were books including on how to learn French or Spanish. Long before I could read them, I would listen to the records and taught myself Spanish. I listened very closely. Before you knew it, I could speak Spanish. Now fast forward as I learned to read and write. I love to read, but I have a short attention span. Admittedly, I have never read a book cover to cover. How ironic, huh? I could speed read and grasp concepts quickly, and I loved numbers. At the time, Momma was a bookkeeper, and I always paid close attention to what she was doing. I learned fractions and decimals from her. Before I even got into the first grade, I was somewhat bi-lingual and mathematically advanced.

I found that first grade was pretty boring to me because I was so far ahead of everyone else. When I was alone in my room at home, I would grab my parent's dictionary and look up different words. The more challenging the words, the better. Then one day, I came across the words "Bitch" and "Bastard" in my research. Now I would be lying if I told you I hadn't heard those words before, but the reality was I heard it a lot on the streets. While I can say that there were a lot of bad words in the dictionary, I can also say that I found out they were actually words with meanings. They were not just cuss words. When I was in the school library while everyone else in class was reading Dr Seuss, I would pick up the dictionary and secretly learn all about every cuss word I could find.

One day, I remember getting called a little bitch in school by another unruly boy while playing on the playground at recess. I guess you could say I outsmarted him by saying, "Do you even know what that means?" Of course when I gave him my intelligent explanation of the word, I never heard that word from his mouth again until this one day. He called me something else pretty bad that I won't mention that was not in the dictionary. He did it again...So in return, I called him a little bastard. Unfortunately, right before I could give my explanation of what my word meant, we were split apart by a recess teacher. Of course we both got drug off the playground by the back of our shirts and called into the office. We were told not to use that kind of language in school or on the playground, and our mothers were going to be called. I said to myself, "Yeah, right." The boy went into the office first. I could hear him pleading and begging, "Don't call my momma!" He walked out in tears. I could only imagine what his punishment was going to be when he got home. Getting whipped with an extension cord from a vacuum cleaner, more than likely. It was my turn next as I sat in the office. This is how that went down...I asked, "Why can't I say that word? It's in the dictionary in the library. That's where I learned what it means. It just means a child born out of wedlock without a father, and that is what he is. So why is it in the library if I can't use it?" Stunned by my definition without calling my mother, I got sent back to class with no punishment. I guess I was too smart for my own good. Sometimes it got me in more trouble, but sometimes it also got me out of trouble.

Like I was saying, the first grade dragged on. This one particular old and cranky teacher was definitely mean as a pit bull at times. She loved to make a kid cry. She enjoyed it, at least that's the way I saw things. If you acted up in class, she would verbally punish you until you cried. Absolutely brutal, I am telling you. After she made you cry, she would then have the entire class chant in unison, "Cry Baby, Cry Baby" to you over and over until there was nothing left of your dignity while you sat at your desk bawling your eyes out.

Have you ever heard of phonics learning? Long before phonics, my first grade teacher had a special way to make us learn. When it came to sounding out words and learning to spell, she had this magical formula of showing us how to sound out a word and then dissect it. For example, the word DOG. She would have the class together in unison say the word DOG... Here is how it worked. She would say, "DOG," as she commanded, "Now class..." We all said the word DOG. As she continued, "Now take the letter D off," and we would all say at the same time the sound OG. Lastly, the letter O came off, and we would all make the sound a G makes, Geee. Funny, as I learned later in life it became known as phonics, but I actually called it just plain boring in class. So one day, the teacher decided she would have a more challenging word for us to dissect. Now she had my attention with a more challenging word, finally. Of all the words in the world, she chose the word GLASS. As she began her instructions, "Take off the letter G." Then, we went onto L. All that was left was, well, you know the word ASS. So in unison, we all said the word ASS. Then we had to dissect the word ASS, too! Do you know what it sounds like when a class full of 1st graders sound out the word aaassss in unison? I guess she thought it was quite comical, but to her defense it was a word in the dictionary, right? I knew ASS meant donkey thanks to my curiosity with the dictionary.

In that respect, she and I had some similarities. She was too smart for her own good, just like me.

As mean spirited as this teacher was, I can say that she did recognize my intelligence. This one time I took a math test, and I could not figure out the answer. It really frustrated me. I knew it had to be between two numbers. I put my final answer down. It was 1 and 1/2, and I used my fractions. During class she called me up to her desk after the math test for not getting a simple answer right. Totally terrified, I was wondering if it was my turn to have the class chant the words CRY BABY, CRY BABY to me. I slowly made my way to her desk knowing what was coming to me. I stood in front of her waiting for my punishment...Waiting for my turn to be called a cry baby by the entire class. Surprisingly, she was actually very polite. She began to ask how I knew to use fractions. I told her that I learned from home and watched my momma use them.

The next thing was she had a very serious conversation with my parents. Apparently, it was recommended that I be advanced in school, to be promoted as I was a gifted child. My parents had other ideas for my future. My parents decided that I would be kept in the classrooms with children my own age, and they would not allow the school to advance me. Bummer, because I was sssssssoooo bored.

## Chapter 10 My first fight

Like I was saying, Momma was a Catholic, not a preachy kind or go to church every Sunday kind of Catholic, but she always tried to do right. We always had a family bible around. As I mentioned before, she was proper and always corrected any slang. She taught me lots of intelligent words, adult words. In the first grade, most of my friends and I got separated from different classrooms or by the lunchroom schedule. School was an array of kids from the streets, and quite honestly, some were pretty ruthless. That was just the way it was. One of the things for sure that was to happen in school was being confronted with a fight challenge. The big thing going around at the time was the saying "Yo momma." Kids would say things along the lines of, "Yo momma is so ugly," or just plain, "Yo momma," and so on and so forth. It was a sign of disrespect and putting down your mother, so of course you couldn't back down. If you did, then everyone picked on you. Then you became a target. My momma always said if this happens, you always try to avoid the fight by outwitting them. When someone said, "Yo momma," I simply could reply, "Doing fine. How about yours?" Funny, there was never any response by that reply when I was challenged, and it quickly diffused the situation. So the day came. This time it was different, and I had enough of the "Yo momma" smack. I got my challenge to make my mark in school. I remember it clearly. I was in the school cafeteria by myself just minding my own business. A group of vicious kids approached my cafeteria table, and I knew I right away it was going to be nothing but trouble by the way the stood and stared me down. It started like this…"Yo momma." This time I didn't say, "Doing fine. How about yours?" I tried to ignore them. Then the challenge got more aggressive.

"Yo momma and yo daddy did it. Yo momma did yo daddy."
In street terms, that meant my mom had sex with my dad.
That was it! It was on Donkey Kong with me. I exclaimed,
"No one is going to disrespect my momma like that! You
stay right here." I happened to see my next older sister
nearby and got her to fight with me, not telling her what all
was said. Having my sister on my side, we stood in
solidarity. Then they said it again, "Yo momma did yo
daddy." I squared off with my fists tight ready to defend my
momma. Firmly snarling with dragon smoke coming out of
my nose, I said, "My momma is a virgin!!!"…I had won the
fight challenge without even throwing a punch, but ready
to…The truth be known, I really thought my mother was a
virgin and would never engage in such a thing. The
audacity!!!!!!!!!!!!!!

## Chapter 11 From the bee stings to the lion

By second grade, I was writing with both my left and right hand and was constantly scolded in class to write with one hand only. I found that very difficult to do. My teacher eventually made me choose which hand to write with. I chose my left hand because everyone else used their right. Then I was told to keep my right hand behind my back while writing with my left all the time throughout that year. Apparently, I was ambidextrous and able to write with both hands. I favored my left hand from there on out and eventually never used the right hand again. I would later learn that I was thrust into a world made for right handed people.

By the third grade, you knew every teacher and every cafeteria lady was armed with a wooden paddle. Each teacher gave their beaten up old paddle a name. Some had writing with marker on them and some with holes drilled in them. They usually hung on the side of the chalkboard behind the teacher's desk, I guess as a reminder. I dared not to even get close enough to one to read what it said or what its name was...That all changed one afternoon. The class was constantly talking over the teacher during lessons as she warned us all. I guess we were restless and continued talking too much. To quiet us down, she told us all to line up along the chalkboard. One by one we had to bend over and hold our ankles as we each got one swat. I watch in horror as even the most ruthless and toughest boys in class walked away with tears of pain in their eyes. It was now my turn. I slowly bent for my paddling. That paddle came swinging hard, and it stung like a thousand bees.

SWAK was all I heard. I couldn't sit back down in my school chair it hurt so badly. I rustled in my seat to find a comfortable position, but nothing helped. When I got home that night, I turned my head over my shoulder before bath time and looked down. I had little red circles embedded in my butt from the holes in the paddle. That's when I figured out what the drilled holes in the paddle were for. The holes acted as suction as you were paddled, creating more pain. I did my best so Momma couldn't see my red circles on my hiney at bath time. If she saw them, I probably would have been in more trouble with her for being disobedient in school. I bet it was three days before I could sit right again.

I have to say even getting paddled by her, she still was my favorite teacher. She really loved teaching all of us and would always bring something new to the class to do. This one day she brought us all a form to fill out. It was for a contest for all the schools in Gary, and our entire class was to enter. Apparently the city of Gary had a mascot, a lion, and he needed a name. I filled out the form to give him a name. The winner would be invited to downtown Gary for a huge celebration. I thought and thought, and then I came up with the perfect name. I named him Larry Gary Lion and turned in my form to her. A week or so passed by, and my teacher had a huge announcement to make. Someone in our class out of all the schools had won third place. To my surprise, I had won third place and was going to be honored by the Mayor of Gary.

The day came for the grand celebration and my recognition. Momma never took me to downtown Gary before. It was a dangerous place. Momma even got her car window shot out once when she was downtown paying for an electric bill. My momma was bound and determined that I was to get my prize for third place. She dressed me really nice and put my hair in ponytails and ribbons. We sat in the car for a while before we were to go downtown. Momma was street smart growing up in the streets of New York and all. She had specific instructions before we left. I was never to make eye contact with anyone as she drove down the main streets of Gary. The doors had to be locked at all times. Also, if we stopped at a stoplight on Broadway street, I was to be the lookout for anyone suspicious coming up to our car. Back then the big thing was stealing your wheels right off your car in a matter of seconds as you sat at the light with four people on each side of the car. I followed her instructions. I remember that scary drive, and I soon regretted entering the contest. You could smell the steel mills burning on the way in. I saw burned out dilapidated buildings, homeless people, bars on every door and window, and a lot of graffiti. Thankfully, we arrived safely without any problems. I was told to sit up on the podium with the Mayor of Gary. As he gave his speech, I was introduced as a third place winner for naming the mascot, and he honored me by presenting a big stuffed lion and an award. The fire trucks, fireman, and policemen were all there. During the celebration, a fireman climbed a huge ladder way up in the sky with a bag. He dropped round clear plastic balls filled with toys and candy for the children. They bounced to the ground, and with huge smiles on their faces, the children scattered everywhere to find them. A band played, and the town was full of loud music and vibe. It was amazing as the wonderful barbecues were smoking and filled the air. I was very proud to be sitting right next to the Mayor of Gary that day.

Even in the city of Gary, people stopped for a brief moment in time to celebrate and to forget about crime to enjoy the moment. It was a huge lesson I learned that day. Even being a crime ridden city and holding one of the most murders per capita in the United States, the people of Gary still loved their city and loved to celebrate, especially with a good barbecue.

## Chapter 12 From sting to string

After getting my first paddling and celebrating with the Mayor and all, the school year ended. I really missed that teacher. Soon I went on to the fourth grade. This teacher was ok. I can't remember anything in class too exciting, but there was this one thing.

They decided to offer a music class learning to play the violin and viola. Of course I wanted to join in. Any excuse getting out of class and learn something new. The best part was I got to take my musical instrument home with me on weekends. Our group practiced each and every week together learning to play classical music. I practiced very hard all year, and the house was always filled with my music as I was learning to play. Toward the end of the year, there would be a school concert at the town hall. I looked so forward to that day. Then the day finally arrived. At noon the bus was leaving to take our orchestra for our big debut. We were told specifically to be on the bus by noon and to not be late. My teacher was absent that day, and we had a substitute. As she read our names for attendance, she came to mine. She asked me if my last name was so and so, and if I had a sister named so and so. I politely answered, "Yes, that is one of my older sisters." As the clock was running on the wall, she began to give the class instructions with work to do. I obeyed and turned in my work with the rest of the class. She called me up to her desk and began giving me more and more things to do, more than the other kids. I told her that I had to be on the bus for my concert with my viola. She simply ignored my excitement with more and more work. I turned in my work again and again to her. I anxiously told her that I would miss the bus soon if I didn't leave. She still would not dismiss me until all of my work was done. It was now 5 minutes past noon, and I went to my locker and quickly grabbed my viola. I ran as fast as I could. When I finally got to where the bus was to be waiting, everyone was gone. My heart sank and with my head down, I slowly made it back to my locker to put my instrument away one last time for the year. I returned to class and told the substitute teacher that I had missed the bus. With a smirk on her face she said, "Well that's just too bad, isn't it?" I walked home that afternoon very sad. My older sister was home. I began to tell her what had happened, and how the substitute teacher brought up her name. My sister demanded to know who it was. Then she said, "I know who that is! I beat her up in school before and she hates me." In that moment, I realized I had been punished by someone who hated my sister. I became the target of her revenge.

That's the first time I found out how cruel adults can be. My next thought to myself was, "How can someone be so cruel?" I worked so hard on learning to play the viola. Even a paddling from school never stung as much as that did. It really hurt me.

## Chapter 13 What do you want to be?

Momma had a way to always cheer me up. Missing the music concert was my first real heartbreak in life, but Momma made it up to me and made me so happy again. Momma loved theater and ballet from her days in New York. She would often take me into Chicago to see the latest ballet. Our favorite play was the Nutcracker. With her love of ballet, she wanted to introduce me to the world of theater. She enrolled me into ballet classes. I got new ballet shoes, pink tights, and a fluffy tutu. She would put my hair in a tight bun, and off I would go to ballet class learning relevés and dancing on my tippy toes. Every week she would take me to a main street which was somewhere between the dunes and entering the steel mills about 15 minutes or so from our house. Every week we went. I looked forward to it so much, and it was just whimsical as a child. My ballet classes ended for one reason or another, and so my dreams of becoming a ballerina eventually came to an end.

That was ok because she enrolled me in gymnastics, too. It was the first time I can remember peeing my pants. I was used to holding it while waiting to use the bathroom living with ten people at home. I guess I waited too long during class. I got lost and couldn't find the bathroom. Well, I had an accident. Reluctantly, I told Momma what happened and was very embarrassed. I told her I wanted to quit. Momma never pushed me into something I didn't want to do, and she agreed. She comforted me and made everything ok again. I guess I never became a ballerina or a gymnast, but I knew I was going to be something someday.

My parents sometimes sat at the dining room table for their morning coffee together. It was a bright and sunny morning as I eagerly joined them at the table. They began an adult conversation as they sat beside me with a serious talk. It began, "Your father and I would like to talk with you. Do you know what you want to be when you grow up?" I answered the question back with, "I am not sure." I knew I wasn't going to be a gymnast or a ballerina. After giving it some thought, I wanted to give them an answer they would be proud of. I said, "Maybe a doctor or lawyer." Honestly, I wasn't giving them a straight answer. The truth was I really wasn't sure what I wanted to be when I grew up, and I had never really thought about at all that much. I always wondered what I would become when I grew up after that.

## Chapter 14 My first encounter with a gang

It must have been about the end of fourth grade when my sister four years older than me was on babysitting duty one particular summer day. I really wanted to go to a friend's house and get out. It had been raining fiercely, and we stayed indoors. Now this particular sister never let me hang out with her. I was a pest to her most of the time. I guess it was because I always took her pant hangers and clean underwear all the time when mine ran out. This rainy afternoon, I was bored out of my mind while she babysat me. I guess she was pretty bored, too. She offered to take me to my friend's house up the road after I begged and begged her. But wait. It had rained pretty badly, and there were nothing but huge puddles everywhere. She grabbed my older sister's car keys to take me. She was not even old enough to drive, let alone think about it. I think she just wanted to ditch me. Without any problem, she started the car and put my twin brother and me in the backseat. Off we went. I told her to wait for me unless my friend wasn't home. Sure enough, she was not home. Anyways, back in the car I went. I guess my sister was not ready to come home just yet from her joy ride with the car. I finally got a chance to hang out with her for a change. Now this car was no prize. It was rigged with speakers that weren't hooked up. One speaker sat on the center hump loosely in the front. Every time we turned, the speaker fell off the center hump. She decided to drive further and further away down to the middle school, which of course was flooded with rain water. As she approached the school fence along the football field, the street was full of water and looked like a lake. In her wisdom to avoid the huge puddle of water, she drove the car on an embankment along the school fence and got the car stuck in the mud. Not only were we stuck, but now we were stuck on school property! We couldn't get out as she feverishly spun the tires. As I look in the rear-view mirror, I saw a gang of people with nunchucks and batons with chains swinging in the air. We were definitely in trouble. I screamed, "Hurry, hurry, a gang!!!" My sister gunned it, and of course we got stuck even more. As anticipated, the gang came up to the side of the car ...Tap, tap, tap on the window. I thought we were dead. "Looks like you are a little stuck there," one gang member said to us. Then with a huge surprise and to our amazement, they friendly said, "We can help you get unstuck." As they put away their weapons in their back pockets, all of the gang members got behind the bumper of the car to help push us out. Even gang members wanted to do a good deed from time to time. Over and over while spinning the tires with the roar of the mucky mud sandblasting the car, it failed. One gang member yelled to my sister, "Step on the gas hard while we all push." With the car rocking back and forth, my sister followed his command and spun the tires furiously with smoke coming out of the exhaust pipe Dukes of Hazard style... Looking back in the rear-view mirror, I could see the gang was entirely full of mud from head to toe dripping wet as they stood up. My sister took off like a ban-chi as we spun away with gritty mud casting in the air behind us. Then they started chasing us on foot with chains in the air as our getaway car roared down the street. They screamed, "We're gonna kill you!" Luckily, we got away. Caked with mud all over the car, she quickly pulled into our parent's driveway. Just as she was making the sharp turn into the driveway, that stupid loose speaker on the center hump in front fell over again. It fell onto the gas pedal, and we drove the car right through the garage and wrecked. If the gang didn't kill us, Mom and Dad sure were going to!!! I mean I hadn't even hatched my egg yet to become a woman, and I saw my life flash before my eyes. We were surely dead meat. With the car half in and out of the garage, she backed up. We knew we were in big trouble as we looked at one another with enormous eyes. Now this garage was never used, and no one could ever open the garage door that was already broken long before we crashed. It was primarily just used for storage. Upon impact, we knocked out a few bottom panels with the front bumper and hood of the car during the acceleration. Somehow we manage to nicely stack the panels back up together, and no one noticed for a couple of years. Of course my oldest "Big Brother" got blamed for it by my parents because as you know, we were way too young to drive.

As expected, my teenage sister who owned the car found out what happened. I mean come on, there was mud all over her car. You couldn't miss it, even though there was no damage to her prize car. We ultimately confessed to her and begged her not to tell Mom and Dad. She knew exactly what happened. She promised not to tell Mom and Dad, but then she did the unthinkable. She blackmailed us! I took the punishment for everyone because it was my idea to go to my friend's house in the first place. I became her maid for the next month. I had to clean her room and get her a glass of water whenever she asked. She always threatened that if I didn't clean her room or do whatever she said, she would tell Mom and Dad on us. I had to take the punishment for a whole month. Yes, the absolute entire month. When it came to vacuuming her room, no vacuum cleaner was allowed.

My Life Single For Eight Hours

"You will pick up every fuzz ball by hand on your hands and knees," she demanded like a queen on a thrown.

Then one day, I got my revenge and was tired of being her maid. You see, this blackmailing sister and I had the same exact voice, and I knew she snuck out sometimes to be with her friends on the beach. So when her friends would call the house, they thought I was her. I decided to pretend to be her the next phone call that came in. Here is how that went down...Ring, ring. "Hello." Her friend began, "We had so much fun last night." I simply replied with, "Geeze, I was so out of it. I don't remember a thing. Did we party too much? What did I do?" From there, I was told by her friend the whole story of my sister's shenanigans from the night before partying on the beach. I went straight to my blackmailing sister and told her I knew everything she did the night before. Then I promised to tell Mom and Dad everything if she didn't stop making me be her maid. At first she didn't believe me, and she called my bluff. Confidently with my arms folded, I spilled the beans to her about everything I knew she had done at the beach that night. Detail by detail. Oh, yes I did...After that, I guess you could say we called it a truce and no one ever told Mom and Dad on each other. As for my oldest brother, I am extending a special thanks for taking one for the team and getting the blame for hitting the garage with a car. Thanks, Big Brother.

## Chapter 15 What are sisters for anyways?

Although she tried to blackmail me, she wasn't always a bad sister. If you could picture this sister, she would be an epiphany of an angel with miniature devil horns hidden under her hair. A strawberry-blonde spitfire. Besides, she always had to babysit me all of the time when she was a teenager. She really resented that sometimes, but other times I was her pal. I was a handful always getting into all sorts of stuff. You could double that with my twin brother. I was just curious, that's all. Long after her hanging me on a hook by the back of my t-shirt in the backyard to keep me from getting into things and to teach me a lesson, I had to forgive her for blackmailing me...Even though she left me outside hanging there long enough for as a stray dog to show up and start sniffing my feet as I hung there all alone, she was forgiven. I thought that dog was going eat me.

I had almost forgotten that story with the dog until I started writing. There were plenty more. Long before I could ever remember, my parents lived on a farm and had a fruit stand when I was a toddler before moving to Gary. Anyways, my oldest sister had a horse named Star back then. Long after Star went to heaven many years later, my spitfire sister always wished Star was hers and still had some of Star's old horse riding equipment in her room. When she was on babysitting duties in Gary, there were a few occasions when she used to put Star's old strap on my twin brother and me. She would tighten it around our waist while spanking us with the loose part of the strap for getting out of hand. We couldn't get away while she spanked us.

My sister later in life revealed to me that she had deeply regretted being so mean to us as kids by doing that to keep us in line. I was never mad at her for spanking me.

She was always just mischievous as a sister, that's all. I had to remind her of the old family stories that she also took Star out for rides without permission long before we had taken her car out without permission, too. The apple doesn't fall too far from the tree. Honestly, she would never let anything bad happen to any of us. She pulled me out of the fire when I fell, remember? Now that is one hell of a sister to have, wouldn't you agree? How could I have ever, ever stayed mad at her for anything?

My spitfire sister may have blackmailed me, but she also was the first sister to teach me about the birds and the bees on the beach. As I grew old enough, she asked me one day if I wanted to learn about French kissing. Curious, of course I wanted to know. She took me into her bedroom and she got out some old records. You know, the old kind with a big hole in the center about the size of a quarter. She handed me a record and told me to put it up to my face as she held hers across the room. I held the record up to my face. Now the records were smaller ones. When you put it up to your face, you could see over the top. I carefully followed her instructions. She stuck her tongue through the hole in her record from across the room and told me to do the same. She began, "Now take your tongue and move in a circle to the left. Then go backwards and spin your tongue to the right."We practiced and practiced until I learned how to French kiss the right way with records. Over and over we practiced until she finally graduated me.

Now if that sister wasn't in charge, another one was. If Momma had to work late, my sister who always saw me as a pest and wanted nothing to do with me was usually in charge. This was the same sister that had driven the car through the garage. Momma would write out all the dinner plans on an index card with specific instructions. This sister as you know was just four years older than me, but what you don't know is how terrible of a cook she was. I mean the burning water kind. Unfortunately, Momma had left "The Great Chef" in charge a lot. We had a long table with ten chairs, and it was always nicely covered with a pretty table cloth and a plastic covering on top. Momma left a recipe with instructions on how to make pancakes one night. It was going to be a real treat for a change. Anyways, my sister began her recipe with flour, eggs, and so on. She messed up the recipe and kept adding more flour, water, and then more flour again until all of the flour was gone. It sat in the bowl like a clump of children's play dough. Hard as can be. She decided she would roller pin out the pancake dough and fried them in a pan anyways. They were awful and had no taste with each side burned. She handed me my plate to eat filled with her garbage meal. She said, "It's this or nothing." I decided to grab the grape jelly out of the fridge and doused my play dough with as much jelly as I could find. The center wasn't even cooked all the way. Now mind you, there were foods I didn't like, especially green beans. The best thing about a having a German shepherd in the house is that he ate everything, mostly scraps. I could always count on our German shepherd to eat all of my throwaways that I secretly tossed to him under the table. It was pretty easy to do with the tablecloth hanging down so long and all. I couldn't stomach those burned pancakes of hers. I put them in the dog bowl and waited for him to gobble them up.

True story, you couldn't even get the dog to eat that crap even though he would eat everything else. He even ate my green beans under the tablecloth for heaven's sake...I waited for him to eat the pancakes while she was still busy in the kitchen making her next glorified pancake. The dog sniffed the pancake in his bowl a couple of times, backed up, and then walked away with his tail between his legs. He ate anything and everything, but not this time. The pancakes were that bad. I hurried up and flushed it all down the toilet, pretending to eat it. I went to bed hungry that night, and many more nights whenever she cooked.

Unfortunately, "The Great Chef" would cook for us a lot throughout the years as the smoke sifted out of the kitchen. One day as she was cooking a couple of days before Christmas, a loud alarm sound came out from under the tree. As her smoke sifted through the house, we opened windows to air it out. We still couldn't find what this alarm sound was or where it was coming from. As we navigated our way past the dark sift and smoke, we found this gift wrapped under the Christmas tree. That was where the noise was coming from. Apparently, my dad got a new smoke detector for Christmas waiting for him to open it on Christmas Day. We opened Dad's present after shaking it a bit. Let's just say that every time she cooked, my twin brother and I would hide the smoke detector under the couch cushions ahead of time. Don't even get me started on her spaghetti!

My Life Single For Eight Hours

## Chapter 16 My confession and a pastry

The hot summer before the 5<sup>th</sup> grade, the crime in the neighborhood was increasing. Mom and Dad pulled me out of the Gary school system and put me into a private school in Gary. I was placed in a Catholic school for the 5<sup>th</sup> grade, and now I had to re-adjust. It was no longer "Yo momma" or "Yo daddy." It was now "Who is your daddy?" and "Who is your momma?" No more "Yo momma" challenges in school, but a bunch of bad and snobby girls that decided either you were in or out of the click...Or a lot depended on who your parents were. My parents were middle class and hard working people scraping sometimes everything they had to send us to private school while feeding ten of us. Sometimes they had a lot of money, and sometimes they didn't. I always did my own thing and didn't want to be part of any click, that's for sure. They were a bunch of snobs in uniforms, and that's the way I saw it. Totally outside of my usual schooling. I just didn't fit in, or should I say wanted to fit it. Most of the teachers were armed with long rulers. If you got out of line, they would crack the back of your knuckles with it. Sitting up straight was a must with no slouching in your chairs. I always had bubblegum on me. I once got caught chewing flavored bubblegum in class. As a punishment, I had to have it taped to my nose all day in Catholic school in front of everyone. It was a huge wad of watermelon flavored gum, and it was so big that it wouldn't stay on my nose. The teacher ended up putting 5 or 6 pieces of tape over it on my nose to keep it in place. It was hot in class and the gum just kept sliding off and dripped on my schoolwork all day long. It was disgusting punishment. On the brighter side of things, one good thing about Catholic school is you didn't have to figure out what to wear to school that day. It was always the same uniform. I was so glad I didn't have to do to as much laundry for school anymore in the dungeon. I must say, the best part of Catholic school is getting out of class to go to Church for confession. In my mind anything was better than boring subjects, right?

...I admit it. I was an addict. I was addicted to the arcade game of Ms. Pack-man and bubblegum by then. We had a local game room behind the grocery store, and that's where most of us hung out. I was always challenging myself with this game, but it wasn't free. A quarter a game doesn't go very far on 50 cents a week allowance and a 25 cent raise. I began helping myself to quarters from two of my sisters. One sister had her tip jar as a waitress. The other sister was collecting money for a charity for children with cerebral palsy in a milk carton. I know, that was bad. But isn't that what addicts end up doing by stealing to get the rush? I couldn't act like I didn't know what the milk carton was for. I mean you couldn't miss the disabled child on the cover of the carton with crutches asking to donate with a big eyes looking at you. I took the quarters anyways, and I knew better. After finding a coat hanger, I wedged open my sister's milk carton full of quarters she had collected for the children with cerebral palsy. I carefully put it back on her nightstand. Next, I put my older sister's tip jar back in her closet in its secret hiding place. I had enough quarters each week to keep playing the game and to get to the next challenge.

Like I was saying, in Catholic school you get dismissed to go to confession during the school day. Now I had never been to confession in my life. I never even knew what to expect. Sitting in a dark closet with a priest wasn't exactly what I had in mind to get out of class, but anything was better than boring subjects, right? I then asked my classmate what happens during the confession. It was explained that if I confessed my sins, I would be forgiven. Anyone reading this, you know I needed that for sure. Now it was my turn to confess. I enter this big black box facing forward. The priest was on the other side of this screen facing forward in the pale lighting and he asks, "Child, have you sinned?" Staying in character, the priest never faced me and we both stared forward for my confession. Now a line of kids are waiting behind me outside the box, and I have to confess to be forgiven. I proceeded to tell him that I had sinned. I told him that I had stolen quarters from both my sister's tip jar and some from the charity milk carton for cerebral palsy to play the game Ms. Pack-man at the arcade. All of the sudden in his furious voice, he broke his priestly character, turned to me, and yelled, "You did WHAT???" ...What, what, what, what, as it echoed slowly through the church full of kids. I sheepishly turned back at him staring at me in shame, and I repeated my confession to him. He said, "Child, you are going to HELL!!" Strangely, in that very moment I said to myself, "Priests cuss, too?" That was when I realized he meant the literal dictionary term. You know, the fire and flames kind of place. Remember, I looked it up in the dictionary. He demanded, "You must repent." He further demanded that I say the prayer Our Father 25 times and the prayer Hail Mary 15 times before I could leave the confessional. Now I was at most a novelist Catholic, and I did not know the Hail Mary prayer yet. It took an hour and half, and he had to say the prayers with me and make me repeat after him 15 times the Hail Mary prayer. He was not happy with me to say the least. Meanwhile, outside the confessional the other kids were getting restless. You could hear their whispers, "She's been in there a long time. Yeah, 'cause it must be really bad." Finally, an hour and a half later after my last Hail Mary prayer, I was released from the dark box. I had to walk past every kid standing in line staring me up and down as a sinner! The walk of shame. I did the crime and paid my time. Let's just say I never did it again, and the game of Ms. Pack-man became a thing of the past. Not to mention my addiction to bubblegum was gone, too…I wasn't about to tell the priest that story. I guess you could say I decided to take my chances of going to hell or not over getting free bubblegum.

My twin, The Great Chef, and I took always took the city bus back home after school. We would sit at the corner of the Catholic school and catch the bus to drop us off at the grocery store by our house. It was maybe a 15 minute drive or so at the most from home. I always had my bus money on me. This one particular sunny day after school, I was really hungry. It was a long day at school, so I decided I would get myself a treat at the bakery nearby. I told my twin brother that I wasn't going to take the bus, and that I would be home later. I wanted to take my bus money and buy a pastry at the bakery instead. My brother thought it was a bad idea and tried to talk me out of it. By then, most of us walked in groups for safety. I said that I would be fine walking home. I knew how to handle myself, and I was pretty street smart. I was going to walk along the main drag, walk through the park, and take the short route along the shoreline. Still in my uniform with my books, I got my pastry and began to walk home on the main street. All of the sudden out of nowhere, I heard wheels screeching to halt. Two men in a car cut me off and slid their car right in front of me and opened their doors. They blocked me in. With their engine still running, they quickly jumped out and attempted to abduct me with pure evilness in their eyes. I outwitted them and pivoted just out of their reach. My legs were faster than a bolt of lightning as I ran away nearly escaping their vile clutches. I ran like I had never ran in my life, and I was absolutely terrified out of my mind at what just happened. I ran to the safest place I could find which was the post office. Out of breath, I began to beg for help from the clerks at the post office. They tried to calm me down and asked exactly what happened. I begged them to let me call home and use a phone. I called home and my caring spitfire sister answered. I told her that I was going to walk home going through the park instead of the bus, and that some men tried to grab me. She told me on the phone that the park was a dangerous place, and I was never to walk in that park alone. She was very upset, as you can imagine. I told her that I had not even made it to the park yet when it happened. She scolded me for being so careless and walking alone. I explained that I was on the main street, and the men tried to get me there, not the park. I soon got picked up at the post office and was driven home. Gary was definitely progressing as a more dangerous place day by day, and the crime was getting closer and closer to home in the dunes spreading from downtown. I wasn't punished for being so foolish. I was further protected by my parents.

My Life Single For Eight Hours

## Chapter 17 Moving to the Country

Mom and Dad had their financial challenges, but things were looking up for Mom and Dad. With crime getting pretty bad before the 6th grade in Gary, they decided to move the last three children at home out to the country. I was now out of Catholic school and in a public school system once again. It was definitely a culture shock. I can say that people in the country life were humble and hard working people. They were really nice people. There was never crime to worry about, ever. I mean people didn't even lock their doors! HUH? Sometimes, Dad would take me to the local truck stop while he drank coffee. I always ordered vegetable soup as he explained the latest technology to me. It became our regular hangout together with the truck drivers. He would sketch diagrams on our napkins and show me how electricity worked. I had everything a kid could want. I had an in ground pool, and I even had my own horses. Country life was as a shock to the system, but somehow I really enjoyed my alone time with nature and my horses out exploring my new surroundings. I had two horses named Otto and Akiem and showed them at the local county fair every summer and at local rodeos. As I rode my horses, they were my keepers. They warned me of any kind of danger by watching how their ears would perk up or turn a certain way. I would say to my horse, "What's up boy? What do you sense? What is it?" Usually, it was a rabbit or small animal in our path. Horses get very attached to their riders, and there was an unspoken language as we bonded. My horses had to trust me, just as much as I had to trust them. Akiem was my Arabian horse, and together we were fearless. I rode him everywhere. We were fast as could be together, totally fearless I tell you.

Dad was fascinated with the Amish people that lived close by and took the family to an Amish auction where they sold animals and bought me Otto. He was a young Quarter Horse, and Otto was barely broken in to ride. He threw me off a couple of times, but I trained him every day until he fully trusted me. I would sing to Otto on our long rides though the countryside to calm him. He wasn't as fast, but he was a great show horse at the fair. We won lots of blue and purple ribbons. My horses became my ride, and I even learned to barrel race with both of them. The best thing was I could get out and explore by going on rides for hours and hours. I proudly showed them both at the county fair as I made lifelong friendships with other locals. Akiem and I won the flag race, and he was the fastest horse in the county one summer. I even entered a hog wresting match during the fair with a group of girls, and we beat out all the guys and won a championship. Yes, I wrestled hogs in the mud!

While riding, my dad would come home and pass me with his car and stop. He would take off on my horse and flew like the wind by horseback with his jacket fluttering behind him. My dad really enjoyed the horses so much, too. Shimp on the other hand was my twin brother's horse. He was an Appaloosa and very mischievous. Shrimp kicked my dad in the knee one time while in his stall. My dad didn't punish Shimp or get mad at him. Instead he got a handful of grain to feed him, and gently bonded with him. It was really something else to see how much my dad loved animals.

Neighbors lived pretty far away for the most part. My dad thought it was a good idea to go down to meet one of our new neighbors. My dad was a humorous guy always telling a funny joke. One day he decided to go down and introduce himself to the new neighbor with a great polish joke. Well, that's how he found out our neighbor was polish. Despite a rough beginning, our families became good friends and always watched out for one another.

One day a young man came down our driveway on a horse. He was another neighbor a couple miles away. He saw my sister, The Great Chef, riding her horse named Savannah. By then my sister transformed from an ugly duckling as a pre-teen into a beautiful swan, and she was a stunning sight to anyone who saw her. He introduced himself to her. He became a regular rider with us right from the beginning. My sister and I saw him once before at an auction, and he looked a lot like the actor John Travolta. My sister had a huge crush on Travolta. Her prince charming just showed up on a horse. The next day he was to come back over for a ride with my sister again. She asked me to come along on the next horse ride with the new neighbor the very next day. I was suspicious. That was the first time I can remember her wanting me to hang out with her ever in my life! Remember, I was her pest? She confided in me that she didn't remember his unique first name and needed my help. The plan was to introduce myself by name and he should give me his name in return. Sounded simple enough. I told my sister that I had her back, and not to worry. She finally wanted to spend some time with me, and I could show her my loyalty as her baby sister. As we all three rode our horses together, I introduced myself as planned. All I got out of him was the response, "Howdy." We continued to just ride. Darn it, not good. I didn't get his name for her. They started dating, and it was a whole month before she ever figured out his name. Yes, my sister was dating him without even knowing his true name for the rest of that month.

He eventually proposed to my sister, apparently without her making one single meal for him before he married her later on...Anyways, our love of horses bonded our sisterhood from there on out. We always had each other's back after that, and I was no longer her pesky little sister.

It was a great time in my life. Mom and Dad would drop my brother and me off at the local roller skating rink on their date night. Dad even showed me how to drive a tractor and how to target practice with a shotgun and a 22 rifle. Now being left handed and all, rifles are a bit tricky. When the shell casings come out, you have to the casings come out past your face instead of away. If you are left handed reading this, you know what I mean by saying it's a right handed world out there...I was taught safety first and foremost. Dad would set up cans, and we would practice my shooting. I got pretty good at it, I must say. One day "The Great Chef" was pushing the lawnmower and a big old snake came out of the grass hissing at her. She came screaming, and I got Dad's 22 rifle out. In one shot, I killed that ugly snake. Not too shabby, huh? Then this one day when I was shooting with Dad, something went terribly wrong. As I pulled the trigger aiming at my target, the bullet somehow got stuck in the chamber of my gun. It exploded inside the rifle as I fired it next to the side of my face. I reached up to my face with my ear still ringing. Dad quickly grabbed me with extreme concern in his eyes to immediately aid me. I thought I had just shot myself. He looked me over thoroughly and checked me from head to toe. Luckily, I had only a few minor burns and couldn't hear for a couple hours. It scared me so badly, it was years and years before I picked up a gun again after that.

Anyways, there was always plenty to do other than shooting guns. I had every animal you could think of including rabbits, ducks, a dog, cats, and horses. Then there was my pet raccoon named Rascal. He was an orphan and was raised from a baby. A man and his wife gave him to my dad, and he became mine. Rascal would greet me every morning before getting on the bus for school. His favorite food was the cereal Lucky Charms. I always had a handful for him every morning. Rascal and I would pal together as he rested on my shoulder. He loved the smell of fresh washed hair and shampoo, too. He would take his little hands and grab some of my hair and just smell it in the morning on the way to the bus. He disappeared one day and didn't greet me before the bus came. Just like that he was gone. I never saw him again after that...I really missed my little buddy, but I always hoped he found his own brand new adventure...

## Chapter 18 The slumber party

By now, I was just starting to make friends in my new surroundings. I didn't have a pet alligator or raccoon anymore to show off, so I had to come up with something interesting to share with my new found friends. I was invited to a slumber party with a bunch of girls from my class. We were all 13 and finally young teenagers. How exciting to be invited. This was my first and only slumber party, and I was looking forward to it. Off I went with my pillows, blanket, and my bag of overnight stuff. After doing a facial, having a pillow fight, and popping popcorn, the girls ran out of things to do. I eagerly pulled out my bag of tricks. Yeah, that's right, my sister's old records. I was going to show everyone how to French kiss…Super excitement and giggles rang throughout the room and everyone was on board. As we all sat in a circle in our pajamas, I began to hand out the records with a big hole in the center. One by one, I handed each curious girl their own record. One girl asked, "What is this for?" I simply replied, "You'll see. My older sister taught me this." I gave my instructions to hold the record over their faces. As their eyes curiously peeped over the top of the record and everything was in place, they followed my cues while sitting in the big circle.

Well, you know how the story goes from here. We practiced and practiced until I felt everyone had graduated from their first French class…Never to spoken of again by any of us after that.

## Chapter 19 More education

Seventh and eighth grade seemed to drag on a bit. I can say that the most boring subject to me was history class. I don't know why, but it just was. I always felt that we never learned the whole story of both sides of a war. The teacher wrote on the chalkboard. We were to learn about World War II and its history. I came into class one morning and posted on every wall were photos of dead bodies from the Holocaust. The entire week we were going to talk about all of the atrocities. It was really overwhelming. At the end of our lessons, he always said that if we had any questions to raise our hand. I finally did one day. I guess I was pretty upset with him that I had to look at piles of dead bodies all the time. I began to ask, "Didn't Americans kill people during the war, too? Why don't we see those pictures on the walls?" I continued without an answer from my history teacher, and the kids all gasped as I spoke. I continued with questions like, "What are other country's commodities? What do they grow? How do they live? Why can't we learn about that, too?" I argued that not everyone could be bad from the other side. I could have cared less if I didn't ace the class. That was the first time I could remember getting a poor mark in school.

The teacher knew it was true what I was saying. I mean come on, I was from Gary, Indiana, and not everyone was bad there either...Let's hear all of the history and not just part of it.

## Chapter 20 A different kind of school

In the eighth grade Mom and Dad took plenty of trips with us into Chicago. Sometimes we were in Chicago after visiting grandparents on my dad's side in the neighboring small town. Mom loved window shopping in Chicago. This one particular time, Mom and Dad took me for a surprise trip to Chicago right as my freshman year in high school was to begin. My parents enthusiastically wanted to enroll me in a modeling school in Chicago. I was excited and eagerly agreed to their plan for me. The next trip, I brought a small portfolio to the school. Nothing fancy, just a few snapshots and a resume. All over the wall were famous people who were originally from Chicago like Raquel Welch and some others. The school gladly accepted me. Next, we had to make another trip in for a tour of the school. As Mom waited for me, I was told I had to tour alone. Puzzled, I followed the woman taking me to each room set up for me. First, she took me to a room with a bunch of books stacked everywhere. She began, "These are for when you place them on your head for poise. You will be training with books balancing on your head and learn to walk straight and poised." Then, the next room they had a dining room set up. They had a round table and lots of fancy silverware perfectly lined on each side of the plate along with crystal glasses. She began, "This is the room you learn to eat properly." With tons of forks and spoons all lined up next to the plate, I was confused as to why there were so many. She explained that I would be learning about all the forks, spoons, and knives for each meal and master etiquette when dining with guests. She began to explain that when I met with talent scouts, I would need to be prepared with dining skills when they sent me to New York and Los Angeles. WHAT??? I wasn't about to go anywhere without my parents, that's for sure. The final straw for me was when she asked if I liked chocolate. I said to myself, "Maybe there is some hope here before I changed my mind about modeling." She told me that I would not be allowed to eat chocolate anymore and gave me a list of the things I was allowed to eat, and chocolate was forbidden! She explained that they wanted to keep my weight and figure always in a certain range. I couldn't get back to my mom fast enough. One the way home, I told Mom that I wasn't going there again. It really was very expensive to send me there, and I honestly felt guilty having Mom and Dad pay so much. Most of all, I did not want to be away from my parents. It was some time later that I told Mom the main reason I didn't want to go was that I did not want to be away from her and Dad. She assured me that they would have never let me go alone one way or another to the city of New York or Los Angeles by myself. She said they were always a hair's breadth away my whole life and would never let that happen. I should have known that. Be as it may, I decided my freshman year no one was going was going to have that much control over me. Ultimately, my aspirations to become a model were over before they even began.

## Chapter 21 From skiing to concerts

My parents always took my twin brother and me out on the ski slopes in the dunes for every birthday as far back as I can remember. It was sometime after we moved to the country, and I guess we earned our parents respect by keeping up with chores. To show their respect and trust in us, they purchased tickets for a show for my twin and me for our birthday as our reward instead of skiing. They were not theater tickets, but actual concert tickets. I couldn't believe it! During my freshman year, they took us to Chicago for a live rock and roll music concert. Mom and Dad were evolving into pretty cool parents as I grew into my teenage years. While my brother and I were dropped off at the concert, Mom and Dad had date night in Chicago. They made arrangements to later pick us up after it was over. I had never been to that type of theater. It was packed with tons of people, and my brother and I were just beside ourselves in the world of rock and roll. The music was so unbelievably loud, and the cheers from the crowd made your ears ring. It was absolutely electrifying. I gave the lead singer the thumbs up while standing on the back of a chair, and it was awesome. He gave me the thumbs up right back! Of course, it wasn't long before I discovered what else went on in concerts. While trapped between the rows and rows of people, my brother and I could not move anywhere. It was jam packed as we watch the exhilarating concert. It got really smoky as people were allowed to smoke. It wasn't cigarettes we smelled. Oh no, it was marijuana, and we were trapped in the smoke! After the concert, I felt really funny and very different. My ears were still ringing, and everything was in slow motion. Mom and

Dad finally picked us both up as we jumped in the car. They asked, "How was the concert, kids?" My brother and I both looked at each other with glossy eyes, and we simply answered, "It was ok." Seeing that we appeared a little disappointed, my parents replied, "Just ok?" If my parents knew what went on at concerts, they would have never bought those tickets for us, that's for sure. As far as my brother and I were concerned, it just wasn't our scene. We were definitely not on board. We never wanted tickets again for our birthday as you can imagine, but we still loved our rock and roll.

## Chapter 22 The high school years

My freshman year in High School was pretty darn fun. I had it all, horses, a stable, a pool, and lots of countryside to explore. I even honed in on my basketball skills and had my own basketball hoop. I was on the debate and speech team. I was on the basketball team, too. I tried out for the swim team and made it, but found that swimming laps back and forth just wasn't the same as swimming in Lake Michigan, so I dropped off the team. Spanish class was offered, and of course I was in that. I mastered my skills in the Spanish language taking every class offered. I also expanded my creativity in art class.

My parents were constants in our lives. They introduced us to a whole new world with everything that they had to give. With their sacrifices, you could say that we were given every amenity a teenager could ever want.

…But like many things in life, that all came to a screeching halt in an instant.

## Chapter 23 It was a bad dream

It was my freshman year in high school. I woke up early when Dad was on his way to work before the sun came up. I had another newspaper article for us to read. It was about the world's tallest man, as I recall. I called out his name a couple of times, but he didn't hear me. I told myself that I would show it to him when he got home. I fell back asleep as he left for work. The last thing I remember was hearing him in the bathroom shaving. I woke up again. Now running late for school, I forgot my library books. I had a lost sleep again. It started out with this reoccurring dream I had for a month straight. I would wake up in a cold sweat and just sick to my stomach. Over and over, each night the same dream that had no ending to it. It was my mom and my next older sister crying behind a big glass window. Then the dream would stop. Day after day, I would drag myself into school exhausted. Now mind you, I was a serial offender when it came to returning my library books. That same morning I got called into the office for not returning my books again, so I thought. As the school secretary walked me to the principal's office, I asked her if was in trouble again for not returning my books. She looked at me and never replied. We just kept walking. As we turned the last corner, there it was. Mom and my sister were crying behind the glass window at the principal's office. In an instant, I knew what had happened. That damn dream. In that very moment, I had this firm knowledge that my dad was dead. No one had to tell me, and I knew on my own that he was gone…It was that bad dream, and I finally knew how it ended.

There they were both my mom and my sister crying behind the glass window exactly the way I saw it in my dream. When I entered, Mom grabbed me in big bear hug and said, "A truck driver killed your dad this morning in a car accident." I just stood there emotionless and didn't hug back. I started to collapse as she pulled me back up. I began to shout loudly for the first time in my life the F word and screamed, "Those fucking truck drivers!" It just came out...I never used that word before and certainly not in front of Mom. But I was so angry..........so angry. Dad was dead and there wasn't a thing I could do about it. If only I had called out his name one more time that morning, talked with him, and showed him that newspaper article. I kept that dream to myself and told no one. I felt a lot of guilt like I shoulda or woulda for a very long time.

The next memory of the events that week was going to the funeral hall to see Dad for one last time after my older siblings all traveled in. They let us see him before the traditional wake ceremony that was scheduled for the next day. In a private room for Dad, all eight of us children stood with Mom and entered...No one said a word or even moved. He was still in his body bag zipped up to his neck. All I wanted to do was be next to Dad. I rushed to his side away from the group. I felt his hair and stroked it one last time. I told him softly, "I love you, Dad." My middle brother quietly grabbed me and held me tight while pulling me away. That was the last time I ever got to see his face. I wished I could have stayed with him longer, but that was the way it was.

It was cold the day we buried Dad, and an Indiana snowfall surrounded us at the burial. When it was over, I didn't want to leave. I turned to my mom and said, "Mom, I don't want to leave Dad here. It's so cold here." My dad's brother grabbed me and held me with tenderness. He gently ushered me away as I kept turning back and thinking how much I did not want to not leave him alone in the cold. He did not deserve to be left alone in the cold by himself. All of the world given to me meant nothing anymore. I just wanted my dad back.

As the cold weather turned to late spring, Mom sat me down and explained, "No more paying for horses, pool, or extras from now on. If you want anything, you will have to work. The money is gone, and your dad had no life insurance." I ended up taking a job and got a special permit to work long hours after school and weekends at the young age of 15.

My Life Single For Eight Hours

## Chapter 24 Going to Vegas

Mom thought it was a good idea for me to take a vacation that summer after Dad died to stay two weeks with my spitfire sister who taught me about the birds and the bees. My sister told me on the phone that she even had a pool for me to swim in. She was married to a military man in the Air Force and got stationed in Las Vegas. My sister was a beauty with her long strawberry-blonde hair and blue eyes, and I am not just saying that. She loved the lifestyle of the big city. She worked in a casino, and fit right in with her gold convertible sports car. She took me out late in the evenings, and we cruised the strip most nights for hours with the convertible down under the Vegas lights. We shared stories about celebrities she met. She once told me how a famous stuntman came to town for a stunt show and got his immediate attention with her beauty. She even had another famous actor that did a double take at her, so the stories were told. She was that alluring. While driving her convertible, we shared gossip about the latest celebrities coming to town. Going through more lights on the Vegas strip, she asked me if I wanted to go see something out in the desert. Of course, you know I did. She began to tell me of these crazy arrays of flickering lights behind the Nevada mountains. Most locals knew it was Area 51, the top secret military place no one was to know about, but locals knew. My sister was more of an adventurer than I was. Imagine that? With the convertible down and the desert dust flying behind us, we took off to this single lane road into the middle of nowhere in the desolate desert and waited for the sky to turn dark miles away from the Vegas strip. The desert gets cold at night, and I was shivering from the drop in temperature. We approached a warning sign and fence that said no one was allowed past that point. We parked outside of the warning sign. She told me stories about her neighbor who was in the military. He would be blindfolded, and he was never told where they were taking him. She knew it had to be Area 51. We patiently waited in the darkened desert. Sure enough, strange lights blasted up from behind desert mountain top as the outline of the mountains glowed. I just wanted to go home. I was cold, and it frightened me to death. I begged her to take me back home. I knew we shouldn't have been there, at least not that close. We ultimately drove home, and I don't think I slept a wink that night.

While on my vacation, we went to visit her husband one day on the base. He was in charge of all of the parachutes and equipment for the Air Force pilots. While we were waiting for him, I got to see some of the equipment and thought they were really cool to look at. With my sister and I being full of adventure, we started playing around and found the pilot's helmets and tried them on. Her husband laughed a bit, but told us to put them back. He snatched them away from us and took all of our fun away. Good thing. It probably wasn't a minute or two later, a big shot walked in. He was a General with several stars on his shoulders. The General was coming to get his equipment for his flight. I had never seen my brother-in-law look that extremely nervous. Actually, my sister and I saw it as an opportunity to meet a celebrity. We had our camera and asked if we could take his picture. Not only did he say yes, but he wanted us in the picture! As my brother-in-law took the picture, my sister and I put our arms right behind the General's back and his behind ours. We posed for a picture with the General that day. It was a spectacular vacation and helped me forget about home for a while. The casinos even let me play slots under aged at the time. I hit the 777, and I was told I could not keep the money. The casino personnel let me gamble right in front of them and spend my money until I won. I have to admit, I was having a great time. I was 15, but I didn't exactly look it. It was 110 degrees in Las Vegas at the time during the day, and the heat was unbearable. My sister had a pool all right and handed me hose to fill her kiddy pool that was knee deep to try to beat the heat. She was definitely a lot of fun to be with though, and I guess she felt bad that she had fibbed to me a little bit about having her own pool. She surprised me and snuck me out one night to go to a real pool. We snuck in and skinny dipped in the dark. So my last night in Vegas, I skinny dipped for the first time in my life.

## Chapter 25 Back to reality

After coming back home to the country from Las Vegas, I for sure wasn't going to tell Mom all things that went on. It certainly made me forget about all the bad things at home for a while. My middle brother moved in with us out to the country. He sacrificed and left his life on the beach to help Mom out and all. It was nice having my caring brother around again. Mom had offered me her old Vega car that wasn't running and just sitting in the grass by the old horse pasture before I got my license. By then I knew how to drive. We had a tractor and an old pick up truck with a stick shift that we drove around the property out to the old pasture fields. Not to mention Dad let me take his car down the road a time or two before he died. He always warned me of the very spot where he died by telling me to always be careful there when I got my license. My older brother and I pulled this beat up car into the garage. With his help, I began to learn more about cars. I entered a speech contest and won, so I had some money to paint my car. I was to get my driver's license that next year and graduate to driving. The new job I got at the part store and repair shop was perfect. I advanced from cashier to parts girl. My manager saw my potential and gave me a chance to prove myself. Alternators, fuel pumps, you name it...I could look up the part for you. The best thing was I could buy all of my parts for my car at a discounted price. It had a Holley carburetor and a cherry bomb muffler. When I saved money each week for a new part, my middle brother would help me to put it on. I entered another speech contest and won $100 and bought my very first tool. I bought a sander, and every night you would find me out in the garage after work and school sanding away. Yeah, she was my baby. When the sanding and painting was all done, I actually used my car as an art project and brought it into the garage at shop class during school. I put my own pin striping on it. I got an A+ for that art project. No one had ever done that before according to my art teacher. By the end of that school semester, I was driving her. It had a few problems. The driver's side door always flew open when you turned corners too fast. We fixed that. There was still the hole in the floorboard that needed to be patched, but hey, she drove. Anyone in the backseat would have to straddle the hole and pavement going by. It had a CB radio in it. I guess you could say I made my peace with truck drivers with Dad and all. "Not everyone is bad," I had to remind myself. With a CB in it, I could talk to truck drivers if I wanted to. I used the handle Little Bear. The truckers would warn me if a county mounty was around, which was CB talk if a police car was nearby. They always watched after Little Bear in the red Vega, and they became my friends on the CB. I would get on the CB radio and say, "Hey, this is Little Bear. Any county mounties out there?" That was my middle brother's idea of a cell phone back then as it was about ten miles into town for my job and school. It was pretty cool though. My new found freedom was the best thing that whole year. I loved to work on my car, order parts for customers, and see what the latest radio was on display hoping to buy one. It still had an AM radio in it, but I didn't mind. I guess you could say that was really when I started to enjoy cars and their latest technologies. Plus I had my middle brother always teaching me more about cars and being my protector on the road.

It wasn't long before I wanted to see what it had. I pushed its limits more than a couple of times and turned it loose like when I used to ride my horses. I never knew how fast I was going because the speedometer was broken. Most of the time, I guesstimated. I was running late for work, and of course I knew I was going fast. Really fast. I wasn't on the CB that morning, and I passed a county mounty. I looked back in my rear-view mirror, but he was long gone. So I went on and sped up some more. Yep, the blue and red lights started flashing behind me, and I got pulled over. He asked, "Do you know you were speeding and how fast you were going?" I honestly couldn't give a straight answer. I politely replied, "No officer, I don't know how fast I was going. My speedometer is broken." Taking my license from my hand he said, "Young lady, you were going pretty fast. I clocked you at 92 miles per hour, and it took me a mile and a half to catch up to you." He let me go with a warning, thankfully. Then he told me to get my speedometer fixed. I just had this thing for speed, and actually I was pretty impressed my car could even go that fast with all the new parts I put in it. I didn't tell Momma of course. Would you?

My junior year in high school I was still working at the part store driving my car back and forth. I came home to a package. It was a package that was full of brochures of girls in a pageant and an entry form. I never knew why they sent it to me. It was quite lengthy. I filled out all of my awards and accomplishments. It was not your ordinary pageant, and I had to have a certain GPA with my grades to even be considered. I sent if off and the next package arrived. I was nominated to be in the pageant with lots of the top girls in the state. Now Miss America was the pageant of the day with its popularity back then. This was called the Miss American Coed Pageant. It was a pageant based on grades, leadership, beauty, as well as your accomplishments. I had won many awards on the speech team and showed my horses over the time. My schooling GPA wasn't at the top of the class, but it was pretty good. I was on the honor roll. I never had time to study like I would have liked to working and all. Ultimately, I was selected. I won three trophies in that pageant, the speech competition, an outstanding program participation trophy, and a top finalist trophy. I earned a special crown to wear during the pageant by getting sponsors, and only a few girls earned the same crown. Momma bought me a beautiful red evening gown and a new necklace for the pageant. I was introduced to the audience by name and my accomplishments while being proudly escorted by my twin brother. I knew money was tight for Momma, but just as she always did, she made my week in the pageant magical. During the pageant, I learned a little trick along the way. I had to put Vaseline on my teeth to keep them from drying out and sticking to my gums because I always had to be smiling. So with Vaseline on my teeth, the last thing I had to do was smile and take my last walk past the judges a few times. Next, they were to decide who to crown as the winner and runner up. The top finalists walked in a huge circle one last time in our gowns to smile and wave at the judges who made their final choices. I was told I was most likely to win by my peers, and I was ecstatic to be revered so highly by the other girls. As we made our final round, something happened. My dress got snagged on the stage, and I had to un-snag it right in front of the judges. It was snagged like a fish on a hook. The beading on the bottom of my dress was caught.

Well like I always said, life changes in an instant. I didn't win that day, but it was a highlight of my high school years and an honor to be a state finalist.

I pressed on in high school and worked at my job at the part store. The year flew by, and I finally became a senior in high school. Other students were getting their acceptance letters for college, and I envied them. There was no money for college, and I was getting restless in the country.

My Life Single For Eight Hours

## Chapter 26 I graduate and move

The day finally arrived, the best day of all, and I graduated. By then I had been dating someone for about two years and got married. It was decided that he needed a better job and something to support us if we were to get married, have a family, and one day get our college degrees. Eventually he joined the military, and I followed.

At the young age of 18, I got married at the town's local courthouse and felt like a change from the country was what I needed and wanted. No need for a real wedding. There wasn't money for it anyways. Ready to move on to my next adventure, I was bound and determined to get a degree. Mom told me there was no money for college to help me. By this time she was a full time nurse trying to keep it all together and to just keep a roof over our heads. I wasn't missing out on schooling and made the decision to move out and pay for my schooling on my own. I thought maybe he would get stationed somewhere in the states, but I was so wrong. We got stationed overseas, and I left the country life for a new life with the Air Force in England.

## Chapter 27 Learning about England

I moved to England with a plane ticket and $500 in my pocket at the age of 18. Of course I had my driver's license for about two years by then. Before Dad died, I already mentioned he let me drive his car sometimes teaching me before I had my license and all. I could drive tractors without any problems, but driving in England was a whole another story. Not only did I have to learn to drive on the other side of the road, but I had to learn to drive with the steering wheel on the other side of the car, too. Yikes! The roads were all very narrow, and the road signs were completely different. Not to mention the thick fog that always rolled in. Somehow I mastered my driving skills and got a permit to drive on the air base. I learned very quickly how dangerous driving was over there. My first experience being on a road, I was passed by an oncoming vehicle. It was just a two lane road. The oncoming car passed and made it into a three lane road. It squeezed between me and another car head on and going very fast. It was insane! Not only passed me, but did it in the dense fog as well! That was just normal driving over there.

In England you are taxed on everything. I mean everything down to the television. Yes, the television was even taxed, and you had to buy a permit for one. I had only 4 channels to watch with the choices being cartoons, a documentary, or British soap operas. That was it. Everything was in metric and Celsius. I watched the weather and it would say it was 17 degrees in Celsius. I didn't really have time to watch TV anyways, but we had a TV permit. Once in a while a van would drive by with a satellite on top monitoring who was watching television. If you were asked, they stopped by and you had to show your permit. If you had a colored television, that permit was more. They actually stopped by the house once and I had to present our permit. There were things in America I guess I took for granted.

We had a slot with a flap in our front door instead of a mailbox. Every week the mailman came to the door as you heard the slot open. Your mail along with the local newspaper landed on the floor in the hallway. My spouse always beat me to the mail each day, until one certain day I got home before he did. To my amazement as I opened the local newspaper, there was a topless woman on page three. WHAT???!!! She was called the Page Three Girl, and every week it was a different woman and always on page three right there in the local newspaper. No wonder he always tried to beat me to the mail. Try that in America.

My Life Single For Eight Hours

## Chapter 28 My troubles

Our military base had two sides with one side having what is called the flight line. The Queen of England owned the road going down the middle of the base on the main street. It wasn't unusual to see protesters on the Queen's road marching with their signs up not wanting our air base to be there. With the air base split in half, you could drive to the fight line. Basically the flight line is where all the military fighter jets are kept and launched. Approaching any check point they would have a sign up Alpha, Delta, etc. Different warnings were posted Alpha or Delta and something else to alert the members of the armed service and their families of any threat to the base. At some point only certain personnel were allowed and the area was restricted with signs. In England, it is a country well known for its thick fog. I mean sometimes you couldn't see your hand in front of your face. Once in a while a military friend of ours would need a ride out to the flight line which was six miles long in the middle of nowhere. I was happy to drop off a fellow serviceman, but I had never been out to the flight line before. We got to the check point, and I dropped him off there in the dense fog as he quickly disappeared into the blurry mist. I began to make my turn around in the thick fog, and I heard someone yelling at me to stop. It was a military police officer, and I was barely able to stop and miss him. With his military rifle pointing directly at me, we locked eyes. It was intense. He was aiming for a kill shot. I knew that because I had handled rifles myself. He screamed while holding his rifle for the shot and yelled, "Do you know I have direct orders to shoot you? Do you? Anyone crossing the checkpoint line is a threat to the air base, and I have direct orders to shoot anyone crossing it." I calmly began to persuade him not to shoot me. All I can say is I am alive to write this book. I explained to him that I was simply making a u-turn and did not see the line on the path or threat level because of the thick fog. I made a mistake. With the two of us hidden from sight by the dense fog, he hesitated. For some divine reason, he put his military rifle down to his side and nodded me to go on. He knew I was innocent, and he stood down a direct order. He let me live that day, and I never offered a ride to anyone out to the flight line again. It was at that moment I realized how dangerous things were in England, and how quickly I could get caught up in the middle of it. Someone must have been watching out for me that day.

## Chapter 29 England My first job as an adult

One of my friends on the air base approached me for a job opportunity. She could double her money because she was paid in British money called the pound and could exchange it on the airbase at the American bank. Every pound you could exchange for about two American dollars doubling your money. Plus you got bonuses for attendance. That was a tough one for me. Back in high school, you could have a maximum amount of days of missing school excused a year, and I used each day available every year for one reason or another. Mostly legit, but some not really. I just hated to go to school. I always thought the worst award you could ever get in high school was The Perfect Attendance Award. I never wanted that award for sure. But I wasn't in high school anymore, and I was in an adult world. She said it would be an easy job, and I could make pretty good money. I would end up making upto $21 or more an hour versus my last job for less than $5 an hour back in high school. Of course I was on board. I finally got the details about the job out of her. It was at a chicken factory. Yelk! I would have to help package chickens. Not the glamorous job I wanted, but I agreed because I really needed the money for school.

It was a nasty job. I wore what they called Wellies, or Wellington rubber boots. It was always wet and cold as the chickens had to stay a certain temperature. I have to admit, I was bored out of my mind. Every single day I would process chicken after chicken ready to send to the store. I sat at a table with a partner across from me, and we were each assigned a number. My number was #2. My friend from the airbase sat at another table further away, and her number was

#9. Slaughtered and gutted chickens were hung by their leg by a conveyor above our heads. We were to catch our chicken according to our number, bring it down, and process it for the store. Then we had to put rubber bands on their legs. Sometimes I would miss a chicken, but that was ok because it would come back around again. I got another chance to catch it. I never got to talk with my friend from the base at work because we were always too far apart. Eventually, I came up with an idea on how to communicate with her. I could grab her chicken #9 and stick a note inside for her to read, hang the chicken back on the hanger, and it would make its way back to her table by the conveyor belt above her head. She would grab her chicken and get my note from inside the carcass cavity. Seemed like a brilliant idea at the time. That was just how we communicated all day. It usually read something simple like, "Do you need a ride home tonight?"

I really got super bored this one day, and we started sending silly notes back and forth. I guess you can say we were both young and goofed off from time to time. True to my nature for a fun time, it was a way to make each other laugh to just get through the dreadful shift. Then the day came. I sent her a note a little more shocking than usual. It was a way to greet someone in slang terms from back home in the streets of Gary, Indiana. I wrote, "Hey bitch," in which on the streets of Gary, that actually was a friendly way to greet your girlfriends. Only girls to girls used that slang, and not the boys. If the boys used it, they were calling you a bad name. Anyways, when I sent the note it meant, "Hey girlfriend, what's up?"

Thinking how funny it would be when she read it, I stuffed the chicken with my comical note inside. Well, as the #9 chicken with my note made its way to her, she missed getting the chicken and wasn't fast enough. Her partner across from my friend's table said, "Don't worry! I'll catch it for you," and the chicken was sent off to the store with my note in it. Yes, it was gone with my funny little note.

Two days later they stopped production with a big meeting and everyone gathered around. They apparently got a call from a customer complaining that when they got their chicken out, they found a note stuffed inside with foul language on it. My friend and I stood silently and listened while I covered my mouth trying my hardest not to laugh. The managers of the plant demanded, "Who put this note in the chicken? You better tell us right now. The store chain is threatening to cancel our contract." I think they knew who did it, probably by the way I was trying to hold back my undeniable laughter. I never confessed that day. Ultimately, I quit that horrible job a few weeks later. Oh well. I guess I may have screwed up. But hey, I was young…And who doesn't like a good laugh once in a while.

My Life Single For Eight Hours

## Chapter 30 Making the team

I took a less paying job on the air base, and I worked at the gym. I met a lot of Colonels flying in to visit the base along with all of the big shots. That was better than slinging chickens for sure. Most of the time, I had no problem striking up a conversation with them. I started a jogging club at the gym, and I became a familiar face to most of higher commanding officers. I remember asking one military ranking Major that I had become familiar with if he would tell me the truth about something. Half jokingly I began, "Is there really an Area 51???" I got a response with only a half smirk and a wink, but he was sworn to military secrecy…And we both knew that. A smirk was all I could get out of him. With a smile on his face and me returning one to him, it was what he didn't say that convinced me that he knew more about Area 51. I knew it existed because I had been there myself to see it in the Nevada desert. Now I had corroborated evidence without him saying a word.

While shooting hoop on the basketball courts on the base and working at the gym, I was noticed by someone high up in rank. I was asked to become a member of the Women's Air Force Basketball Team for the base. I wasn't in the military enlisted in the Air Force, but the Base Commander made an exception for me by being a member's relative. After making the cut and the Base Commander making an unusual exception for me, I traveled throughout England to different air bases to play basketball. It was a whole new territory for me, but I loved it. I was not a starter on the team, but I made the team which was what counted to me. Let me tell you, playing basketball over there was like training for the Olympics. We trained with suicide drills, as they were called, while running up and down the courts. They just about did me in. Not to mention, the British women didn't shave their legs or armpits with their tank top uniforms. Sometimes we played other air bases against Americans, but other times we played the British teams. There was nothing feminine about the British basketball players at all. They were big and burly. When they came onto the floor, the gym shook like an earthquake. They were just beasts. Oh, and did I mention, elbowing and push offs in England in European basketball? Yes, I got pretty beat up, and it was just part of playing the game. During one of the practices, I got undercut in the chin by a teammate and had a concussion. The military doctor sent me home with bed rest. After a couple of days, I still wasn't feeling very well at all. We had the European Division Championship Tournament coming up to play against Italy, Germany, and Spain. I was really looking forward to traveling throughout Europe with the tournament in Germany. I had to get well. He took a blood test to make sure I did not have the flu or something. He sat me down in front of him to tell me the results. I was sure I would get a couple more days of bed rest for the big tournament in Germany. He looked at me and instead of more bed rest, he gave me even more shocking news that I was pregnant. I exclaimed, "Pregnant?? What?" In total shock, I walked out of the office with one less concussion and one baby on the way. That's how I found out certain antibiotics counteracted birth control. I looked back at all the times I got so beat up in England on the courts with the falls, the exertion, and the injuries.

Like many tough choices in life, I decided that was the end of my basketball career. I reluctantly stepped down and quit the team never getting to travel to Germany. I called my spouse to tell him I was pregnant, and he actually hung up on me! Can you believe it? He knew I had a goofing around side to me. He thought I was playing a joke on him and didn't have time to play around. His office was next to the Commander's office. So I called again, and it finally sank in. It wasn't a joke.

My Life Single For Eight Hours

## Chapter 31 Stories you never hear

Anyone reading my book that has been in a military family knows that you get your military member in trouble just as much by what you do more that what they do. Now I had moved up in my position from the gym at the airbase and got an accounting operations clerk job for the military. I was in charge of bookkeeping for gas stations, part stores, and repair shops for three different airbases with two in England and one in Whales. I learned gasoline evaporation formulations and ordered all the fuel on the bases. My office was directly across from the base post office. My door was locked at all times, and I had bars on my window. I was doing my job one day, and all of the sudden I heard this bang, bang, bang at the door with a voice saying, "Military police. Open up." He proceeded to tell me that I was not allowed to leave the office, and that the base was on lock down. There were always drills for a threat on base, but this time it was for real. They thought they had found a bomb under a vehicle parked next to the post office right across from my office. I was not allowed by the window to see what was happening, but the bomb squad assembled and did whatever they do. I couldn't see anything going on, and I was scared out of my mind. After hours locked in the office, all I wanted to do was go home and hug my baby girl. She was at base housing about 4 miles away with a mother of a military member I trusted to watch her while I worked. Now when you went through the base housing, it was posted what speed limits you can go. It was ridiculous, only 15-20 mph. My car couldn't even idle that speed. Apparently, I was going 5 miles over the speed limit.

By then I was already upset that I had to wait if a bomb was to go off or not, and now I get pulled over. Let's just say it did not go over very well with me. The military policeman ordered, "Ma'am, please roll down your window." I did as asked. He began, "Ma'am, I am pulling you over for going 5 miles over the posted speed limit." I just rolled the window up in his face. He was not happy of course. I rolled it down again and handed him my license as he said, "Ma'am, I am only doing my job." I mouthed off to him and said, "If you were doing your damn job, there wouldn't be a bomb on the base in the first place. Now you want to hassle me over 5 miles an hour!" After that I was handed some type of paper and brought it home. The next morning my spouse was pulled out of his office and had to answer to his Commanding Officer as to why he could not control his wife...I thought, "Control his wife? What?" He was warned that one more outburst like that again, they would revoke my driving privileges on the base. What a crock.

By this time I was going to college with the University of Maryland's European Division where they had campuses overseas. With an accounting job and bookkeeper on the base during the day, I kept up my school work at night. Working and going to school was something I had been doing since Dad died, but now I had a baby. I pressed on and took double accounting classes with a concentration in business, even though it was not recommended to do so. I am proud to say the best part of all was I paid my classes out of pocket with no student loans!

## Chapter 32 My Second Side Hustle

I was living in smaller village off of the airbase and commuted in each foggy day. On this one particular day after work, I was approached by a British girlfriend dating someone in the Air Force. He was a neighbor, and she was my "go to" person with any questions about how things worked in England. They spoke English over there, but Oxford English which was totally different. For example, braces as I knew were for your teeth, but over there braces were actually what we called suspenders in America. In England, the word suspenders was actually for something else, so I learned. Cigarettes over there were called fags, and actually I was offended when someone asked me if I had one this one time. They would ask, "Do you have a fag?" Anyways, when we had conversations, she would educate me on what certain words meant and vice versa. I went to a men's store once to buy suspenders to match my spouse's red tie. I was turned away and told I was in the wrong store. I argued. I told the salesman that I saw them in the window on display and would like a pair of red suspenders to match my spouse's tie. I even said please. I was again told not at that store and to go somewhere else. Honestly, I thought they just didn't want to serve me because I was what they called a Yankee if you were American over there. Yes, sometimes Yank, short for Yankee. If they didn't like you, they called you a Bloody Yank. Frustrated, I told my British lady friend what had happened…She exclaimed, "No! You did not ask them for suspenders, did you?" I thought for a second and I replied, "I simply asked that they were to match his red tie." As she explained, I was actually asking for ladies guarder belts to match his tie. As we giggled about that for a while over a cup of aromatic tea, our newly found friendship began to evolve as were shared our knowledge from each country to one another. She taught me the proper way to make tea the British way, the only way, and I taught her about shaving her legs. Most British women didn't shave their legs or armpits as I learned from playing basketball against them. I explained that shaving was what American men preferred. I taught her that if she was going to date an American, she would have to shave. She explained, "You know dating an American, we don't have the same feminine products over here in England like you have in America," as the conversation continued. Then she asked me for a favor one day. I replied, "Sure, what do you need?" She bashfully asked, "If I give you money, will you pick something up for me from the American airbase?" She asked me if I would be so kind to go on the airbase and buy her some feminine products and razors just for women. I obliged and agreed to help her out as the British locals were not allowed in the store on the base filled with American products. She paid with British currency. The exchange rate for British currency was almost double at the time, one British pound for every two American dollars. I doubled my money, and she told me to keep the change for buying the products for her. I was making a little money by buying douche and women's razors from the airbase on a regular basis for her. It was a win-win situation for both of us. She got her products, and I made money. She told other locals dating the military men. Before you knew it, I was the "go to" lady in the area for some of the locals dating the military guys.

Thus, my side hustle began with feminine products and women's razors for the locals, the Brits, as we Americans called them. Others would tell their friends to go talk to the Yankee, and I was kindly and eloquently referred to as their supplier, The Yankee Douche Lady. Yes, for my side hustle I was supplying women's razors and douche. With my side hustle, I am happy to say that I made enough money to help pay for my school books with no student loans!!!

## Chapter 33 Oxford, I made it

After my baby girl was born, I vowed to keep going. One of my classes in the evening was a speech class. I was in speech class when we were instructed to do a eulogy of someone we knew. We were also asked to bring in examples of our hobbies and talk about them. Of course I did the eulogy for my dad, and as you know one of my favorite hobbies was artwork. We were then critiqued. The instructor said my eulogy was the best he had ever seen to that date in his career, and I felt honored. As I presented my artwork and my speech was over, my professor took me aside and told me how much he loved my artwork and how good it was. Apparently, my professor was involved with the Admissions Department for the prestigious Oxford Polytechnic, also known as Oxford Brookes University in Oxford, England. He quickly recommended me to the head of the art department and made specific arrangements for me to be interviewed by professors in the art department at the university. I lived only eight miles away from Oxford. I brought my art portfolio in and laid out all of my work to be evaluated. I was then interviewed extensively by professors in the art department. The admission process for the university was seriously tough and very selective as I applied.

It wasn't long after that I received my acceptance letter to Oxford in my door slot. There I was in a highly prestigious university in Oxford studying the one thing I loved dearly, against all the odds.

By this time I was now enrolled in two universities, worked a full time job as a bookkeeper and accounting clerk for the military, and had a baby by the age of twenty. If only Dad could be there to see it though. He would be so proud. I pressed on continuing to attend both universities and working that full time job.

## Chapter 34 The Rembrandt and the sketch

Oxford was full of beautiful structures as I eagerly roamed the campus and my new surroundings. I took my classes very seriously. One of the best things about studying art in England is that we got to take side trips to London to study artwork at the National Gallery of Art in London. We would take a class trip by train into London and study a piece of art on display and write about it. We studied things like brushstrokes, types of paint, technique, and etc. I proudly turned in my first paper. To my surprise, I got an average grade. It was a tough university. I was not too happy and approached my professor as to why I got such a poor grade. He explained that my writing did not show enough detail. He further went into great length to tell me that I did not offer any specifics on how the swirls and brush strokes were painted, and it was simply not good enough. I vowed to never let that happen again. I chose a more challenging painting our next trip to London. I chose the Rembrandt painting on display. Curious, I chose it because it was roped off with red ropes for its protection. It was the only Rembrandt of its kind, a masterpiece. They did not allow anyone to be near it or to touch it, but that was as close as I could get with it being roped off and all. I knew I had a paper to write, and I was going to make sure this paper was the best with all the details I could find. Paint, swirls, outlines, brushstrokes, technique, you name it…My paper was going to have it. The problem was when I went to get the details, the ropes protecting it kept me too far away from seeing any details. I leaned over the ropes to get a better look. Now I could finally get some details for my collegiate paper that I had to write. As I leaned in, I discovered some details were harder to find then others. I used a pointed pen while writing down my findings. As I continued studying the painting, I leaned in even closer and closer. I pointed my pen toward some of its elaborate paint lines and magnificent swirls to get more specific details. I probably was less than an inch or two away while pointing my pen towards all of its uniqueness. I mean I knew I wasn't supposed to touch the painting, but I had to get as close as possible to get the details for my paper. Leaning in with my pen pointed right up to the painting, I closed one eye and leveled the pen to my eye. I looked straight down the length of the pen at the paint strokes, just like when I used to aim down the barrel when shooting my dad's 22 rifle. I honed in on my target... Just like when I shot that rifle. Then it happened. With one eye closed, I was so focused on the painting that I didn't realize someone was approaching me. The museum security grabbed my arm holding the pen an inch or so away from the nostalgic Rembrandt painting. He vigorously yanked my arm away nearly stroking my pen on the Rembrandt painting as my arm was pulled down. He scolded me and said, "Ma'am, I would not do that if I were you." Let's just say that I got every detail I needed for my paper and got an excellent grade in art class......But almost got arrested doing it. Not to mention, I almost added my own artwork to the Rembrandt with my blue pen to make my mark in London as the world's latest artist.

Our third trip to London for art class was completely canceled. Remember how I told you England can also be a dangerous place? At that time in England there was a war going on with a group in Ireland attacking London. The members of the opposition to England were known as the

IRA, the Irish Republican Army. They were constantly planting small bombs throughout London. Small bombs were placed in garbage cans along the train subways, or tubes, as they were called in England. People had hands or feet blown right off, and it was a big problem. My art professor canceled our last trip by train and decided we would study something new in class instead...

In art class at Oxford we had to find a newspaper clipping and create what were called thumbnail sketches. Basically, it was a speed version of a quick sketch containing the outline of the article in the form of wavy lines. I was told to pick out a newspaper. When I got to the table, it was 12 foot long filled with piles and piles of newspapers strewn about. I sorted and sorted until I finally just hastily picked one random newspaper out. When I got to my desk and opened it up, there it was! I couldn't believe my eyes...It was a black and white article with a photo of the sculpture Dad and I talked about when I was a little girl and so often referred to throughout the years. The shark in the house sculpture right there! How could that be? What are the chances? There were no such things in my life that were just mere coincidences. I quickly turned to a classmate and asked if this sculpture was in England. His reply shook me to the core, and I could have fainted...Not only was it in England, but it was just a couple blocks away!

I couldn't get out of class fast enough. I drove to the house to see the sculpture with the front of the shark in the roof and its tail hanging out. This shark was so massive. I still couldn't believe my eyes. Just as I remembered it....The same shark that Dad and I talked about when we first saw the photo in the magazine together. Dad promised me one day we would see it together, and there I was in front of it.

So I quietly said to my dad, "I made it, Dad. I made it to one of the most prestigious schools for art. I am standing in front of the art sculpture you promised we would see together. I am seeing it together for the both of us. Dad, I wish you were here to see it with me. It's amazing." Afterwards, I left weeping all the way home...I kept the article and the thumbnail sketch in my art portfolio collection for years, not realizing that I had not actually read through the entire article......Something I would never do.....Because as you know, my dad always quizzed me on all the facts about all the articles we shared. Regardless, during the excitement I had not read the entire thing.

## Chapter 35 My send off

I stayed behind in England to finish my last semester for about a month before moving back to the United States. My plane ticket was purchased, and I was scheduled to leave out of the airport in London. My last two days I was there, I ran into a lady on the softball team for one of the units in the Air Force. She recognized me and started a conversation about how I was leaving. There was a huge air show the last full day I would be in England on our base and a party that very night before the show the next day. She invited me to the party at someone's house off of the airbase in a small village and said it would be nice if I would come...A lot of people from the base were going to be there along with all of the pilots from America, Europe, and other countries who were performing at the air show. Going to a party wasn't part of my plan, but I agreed to go as it was kind of a send off for me. I would be able to say my goodbyes to my friends and acquaintances before moving back to America. It was a huge party, and all of the pilots wore their flight uniforms which identified which country they were from. I eventually found my friends and said my goodbyes. While sitting on the couch at the party, my last friend gave her goodbye to me. I was now sitting alone on this couch. I guess it was time for me to leave. As I stood up to exit, I accidently knocked into a pilot from Germany. To my surprise, he spoke English. He asked, "Are you leaving? Why so soon?" I said, "I am so sorry I bumped into you. I was just on my way out. I have to pack because I am leaving after tomorrow night to go back to America." I found it interesting that he spoke my language, and we began a conversation. We both sat back down on the couch as I started to ask him questions about Germany, and how he became a pilot. I continued with questions about his country, and what it was like there. He wanted to know where I was from. I explained to him that I moved to England from a little town in the country after living in Gary, Indiana. We talked about the fact that there was no speed limit in Germany, and how during his last trip to the United States he got pulled over for speeding. He asked if I was going to the air show the next day and described his plane. He explained that he would be performing at the show. It was a pleasant exchange.

All of the sudden and out of nowhere, shattered glass was flying just about everywhere with a huge crashing sound. Instantaneously in a flash, he jumped up and shielded my body with his own to protect me from the sudden danger. Apparently, the party got out of hand, and someone threw a chair though the front window. He towered over me protecting me from the entire incident as he shook the glass off of his pilot uniform. Here we were merely strangers, and this German pilot instinctively protected me from the flying glass. I thought back to the time I was in history class when I was younger and argued that not everyone from the opposition during World War II could be bad people. His action of making sure an American did not get hurt was a confirmation of what I already knew to be true. I thanked him, and he gracefully made sure I made it back to my car safely. It was really a somber parting of ways with mutual respect.

He gave me his watch as a token of our newly found friendship, as brief as it was, and we both wished each other well. I safely placed it in a small box as a symbolic reminder of a friendship from two different countries that were once considered mortal enemies.

## Chapter 36 Moving back home

As the years passed on after I moved back to the United States, I opened two businesses. The family grew, and I was on top of my game. I had it all. The family I loved, a career, businesses, and eventually became part of the upper class. Bought a big house, a weekend getaway at a resort for the kids, some commercial property, and we had everything. I worked so hard to provide for the family. I indulged one in my favorite things, cars. While most moms drove new practical vehicles for their children, I drove a sports car or the latest unique vehicle no one else had with my children in tow.

You would always find a few things in my trunk of my car...Always. A basketball and fishing rods. I taught my children how to play basketball and challenged their shots. I showed them how to fish and got them their very own rods. We spent many times fishing in the local rivers or back to Lake Michigan. In return, they always had a football and baseball gear ready to go. My boys taught me how to spin a football and pitch a baseball. We would spend countless hours in the yard throwing footballs, even in the winter with foot tracks everywhere in the snow. I would get a hot bucket of water to melt the snow off of their football and join in. They were so much fun to be with.

My children and I shared many stories, so I might as well share one this one with you, too. They always had the best sense of humor. I guess I let the cat out of the bag one day to them about my childhood fear. There is nothing wrong with little humor. They always made fun of the fact that my biggest childhood fear was piggy banks. Yes, piggy banks. I know you are probably laughing a little bit right now. Don't worry. I am laughing, too. Let me repeat the same story I told them. I know I am putting myself out there, but here it goes. Violent storms always rolled over Lake Michigan. It was a stormy night when I was a little child. The lightning strikes lit up my room. Loud thunder made my windows shake. I could swear my piggy bank's lips were moving from across the room, and it was trying to talk during the storm. I would hide under my blankets until it was safe again. I got a lot of heat over the years for that one for sure. I always got a new piggy bank from one of my children for Christmas or my birthday. They always teased me about it. If it wasn't a piggy bank I got, it was something special they made me in school. As I am writing this book, my first son's clay bowl he made me still sits on my desk at home. I collected all of their school papers in a folder preparing to give back to them when they got older. My daughter's artwork still hangs on my wall in frames. I eventually gave them their baby blankets to keep. I'm not ready to give up the school papers just yet, and keep them for myself for just a little while longer.

## Chapter 37 Give me that map

By now you know I have a twin brother. We look nothing alike, but he is a handsome fellow with deep brown eyes and brown hair like our two other brothers. He was a bachelor for the most part of his adult life. Celebrating our birthdays together was always a regular event, even in our adulthood. I had to buy equipment for one of my businesses with a straight there and back trip, all business and not a vacation. It was around our birthday, so he and I agreed to get a rental truck and drive it to New Jersey through Pennsylvania to pick up the equipment. With a rented truck, he pulled in to pick me up. I had a surprise for him. I got two Burger King hats to wear for the road. Laughing, we drove away with our hats on. Off we went through the mountains and to New Jersey. I was in charge of the map while he drove. We didn't have GPS back then, not just yet. I flipped through the map of the United States until I came to Pennsylvania. It was a long state, the longest we had to go through. The truck wasn't much fun anymore. It was uncomfortable and bumpy the whole trip, and we were pretty worn out. Late into the night, I reassured him of our location. He said, "Something doesn't seem right. The mile markers aren't lining up to what you are saying." The next rest stop, we got out to check the map again. I assured him that we were almost there. He abruptly fired me on the spot as the map reader and said, "Look you big dummy! Pennsylvania is folded in half. We are only half way there! You're supposed to be the smart one, Ms Oxford." I exclaimed while scratching my head, "How can that be?" He was smarter than me on a lot of things, and map reading was just one of them. The map of the United States had a one sided map for each state we were to go through including Indiana, Ohio, and then Pennsylvania. Apparently Pennsylvania was too big for one page so they folded it half. The other half was on the back side, and I never saw it. We were only half way there! I guess you can conclude map reading was not in my DNA, and he was actually the smarter one that trip.

Like I said my twin brother was a bachelor, but what you don't know is how far he took his jokes. He was always playing a practical joke, each one worse than the next. We took a second trip. After being given every excuse from my spouse why he couldn't go, I finally just asked my twin brother for our birthday to go on a cruise with me. It had been years since I had a vacation. I was so looking forward to it. We would spend 7 days on a cruise stopping in Mexico. Excited, we drove to Miami to board our ship. He took the map away from me, of course. He showed up with a 12 foot long subway sandwich for the road. It was so enormous that it wouldn't even fit in the car. So he had it cut in pieces for the drive to Miami. It was hilarious. It was such a fun drive, not like the last trip we took. We boarded the ship and headed for the pool fist thing. After a while, we went our separate ways toward the evening venturing around. I returned later to our cabin that evening, and my key wasn't working. I knocked and knocked, but he must have been sound asleep and exhausted from the long drive. I didn't see that as a problem. The ship was open 24-7, so there was always plenty to do for a while with gourmet buffets and a casino even. I was pretty tired myself. After a while I decided I would go back down to the outside pool area and rest on a lounge chair. I wanted to gaze up at the stars in the middle of the ocean for a minute to enjoy the ambiance. I accidentally fell asleep on the chair as I woke up to the sun in my eyes. I returned to the cabin thinking surely my brother had to be awake by then to let me back in. By now all the guest were getting their breakfast platters delivered to their doors, and most are in the long hallway retrieving them. I knocked again. With my twin brother being a huge prankster, he opened the door and said this, "I want a divorce. You slut! You stayed out all night. It's over." Then he slammed the door in my face in front of everyone. I leaned my head against the door gritting my teeth with embarrassment as I slowly growled like a possessed demon, "You open this door right now!" As I heard my brother laughing on the other side of the door, all the people getting their breakfast platters were glaring at me with shame. I could do nothing but stand there in the hallway with the stares. I could have literally disowned him! After a while, he let me in and I said, "Okay, brother, you want to play games with me? I'll get you back sooner or later for that one." He called my bluff and kept laughing. He thought it was so freaking funny. Still growling I said, "That was not funny at all." I was so mad at him, but he just laughed away. To my luck, all these guests are assigned to the same dinner area as us. Night after night for a week I had to sit with these people who thought I was the slut on the ship and that he was my husband that wanted to divorce me!! No matter where I would go, I was recognized.

The ship embarked as we pulled into a port in Mexico. It was a brand new port. Everything was in Spanish, and it was hot out with the sun blazing away. Really hot outside. Everyone from the ship was looking for a soft drink or something else cold to drink. No one spoke any English. Of course I used my Spanish skills and was directed to a farmacia (pharmacy). I said to my brother, "I'm sure we will find something to drink there." We had our camcorder on, and I started to record our descent down the street to the pharmacy. As my recording continued, there were two pretty girls working at the counter. They were smitten with my brother, and he began to flirt with them a little, being the bachelor he was. Even though there was a language barrier, they were communicating all right. With the camera still going and them flirting back and forth, I politely asked in Spanish if the young ladies would be so kind to get my brother and me a cold pop to drink. So they did. I continued my conversation with the ladies. With my brother having no clue what I was saying and with him still flirting away, I asked the girls in Spanish if they could help me further. I began in Spanish with, "We are from America. My brother and I came to Mexico because he has a big problem, and I am here being his translator." With some knowledge of the Mexican culture, I knew that you could buy certain things over the counter without a prescription in Mexico. I further asked they direct me to the shelf to find something. I told them that my brother and I were there to pick up Viagra for his erectile dysfunction without a prescription because he was too embarrassed to go to the doctor back in the United States. With my brother having no clue, he continued flirting with the girls as they both stared at him with complete shock in their eyes…They stopped flirting with him immediately, and my brother was clueless as to why. I told my brother we would be back in a minute. The ladies helped me find the Viagra on the shelf, and we returned to the counter with my brother anxiously waiting. I quickly handed him the colored box of Viagra spelled out in Spanish. He asked very inquisitively, "What is this for? What does it say? "I said, "Oh nothing, but can you please pay the ladies." He reached in his wallet to pay the ladies, and then they disappeared

My Life Single For Eight Hours

behind the counter and looked disgusted. I thanked the ladies in Spanish for helping my brother out with his big problem. Shortly after, we left. My brother asked, "Did I do something wrong to offend them in there? What just happened?" I waited a few minutes, and then I laughed uncontrollably as I told him that he had just paid for his very first box of Viagra, and I got the whole thing on video! Tu shay, twinnie brother.

My Life Single For Eight Hours

## Chapter 38 Follow your gut instinct

A few specific incidents in my life I can say were pretty close calls, aside from everything else I experienced. I was well into my career and running my businesses back in the United States. Most of the time, I was too busy to even take a lunch. There were plenty of quick places to eat, and I sometimes just grabbed what I could and ran back to the office. I remember I was craving a hot dish from a pizza place just two or so doors down less than a minute away. I got in my car to drive there. I hadn't been there in years, but it sounded kind of good. I had my turn signal on waiting for oncoming traffic to make my turn into the pizza place from this five lane highway. As I patiently waited, I got a strange gut feeling and something told me, "You don't want pizza today." As I continued waiting for traffic, I heard that voice again in my head, "You really don't want that today." I had already picked out where I was going to park as I scanned the parking lot. There was a nice open space next to a telephone pole, and I was going to park there and walk inside. Frustrated and irritated with those thoughts, I reluctantly turned off my turn signal and continued on to the next food place and got a bowl of chili through the drive thru. Strangely, as I pulled out to return to the office, it was eerily quiet with only a few cars. That was very unusual. With the opening, I pulled out and proceeded back onto this usually heavily traveled road. I made my trip back to the office and hung up my jacket in probably less than a minute or two at the most. As I looked out my office front window, I saw people running down the street. I mean running! I quickly went out the front door to see what was happening and ran down to the scene. It scared me to death. An airplane had to make an emergency landing with engine failure and landed on the highway, ultimately crashing in the very spot I wanted to park at next to the pole. The pilot's wing clipped the pole and broke it completely in half. He miraculously survived and no one got killed or even seriously hurt. He landed on the highway swerving back and forth to miss a few cars, and his wing hit the pole. He must have been approaching the highway behind me when I was on my return to the office. I never heard the engine of the plane as I drove less than a minute or two back to the office. Then it dawned on me. Of course I didn't hear the engine of the plane…I remembered flying with my dad. When a plane is stalled in mid air, you hear nothing and certainly no roar of the engine for sure…I was spared that day only by a miracle or perhaps something else.

I had just bought a vintage car and I loved her. She was executive gray with a moon roof and stylish. It was right before Christmas when I got her. Of course, I happily showed her off at my mom's that cold Christmas. As the celebration of Christmas was about to end, it was already dark. My next older sister told me she had to go feed her horses, and the kids needed to do their chores. I gladly offered to take her children back home. Besides, they would get to ride in my new car. I put the children in the car and promised to return in about a half hour. I dropped the kids off safely. As I began my trip back to the Christmas party, I approached the highway. It was same one Dad died on, but I was familiar with the road. I finally got to the intersection to make my crossing to the center median of the highway when that funny gut feeling came over me once again. I heard a voice in my head again, "You don't want to go, just wait." A little frustrated, I just wanted to get back to Mom's party. I started to put my foot on the gas pedal, and I heard the voice louder in my head. This time demanding very loud, "No! Don't go!" I quickly put my foot back on the brake to wait for traffic to go by. I thought, "This is ridiculous. There is plenty of time to cross the road. Besides, the semis and cars are safely at a distance." Then in instant, I had this immediate knowledge. I can't explain it, but somehow I knew there was about to be a horrific accident. So I waited. I was waiting for something bad that was about to happen. One by one the semis and cars all went by with their lights on as I waited for the horrific accident to happen. The last semi rolled past me, but nothing happened and all the vehicles were finally way past me by then. Relieved there was no accident, I realized my head and back were both pressed firmly up against the back of my seat. Peculiarly enough, I didn't remember doing that. I readjusted myself and took a moment to catch my breath to gain my composure back. I said to myself, "Now that was the strangest thing ever." With a sigh of relief, I began to put my foot on the gas pedal once again to make my way across the highway to the center median. Then it happened. My car stalled right in the middle of the highway in the traffic lanes in the pitch dark. I couldn't get it started. Over and over no matter what, it wouldn't start. After a few minutes, a man stopped and saw I was stranded in the middle of the highway and helped me push it to the center median to safety. I called my family to tell them what had happened. My two oldest brothers came to my rescue. Apparently after taking a look at my car in the center median of the highway, my brothers discovered it had ultimately ran completely out of gasoline. Further investigating, they discovered the gas gauge on my vintage car was not working properly. They ran down to the truck stop a block away where Dad had died in his accident, and they got a gas can and filled it back up for me. I returned safely to the Christmas party, but I was pretty shook up. I guess you could say someone was looking out for me that night.

I was on my way to the office one wintery morning. That strange gut feeling came over me again and that voice in my head told me to go look for my mother. My mom was pretty independent. No real cause to always check on her, but something kept telling me to keep looking for her. I knew I would be late to the office, but I drove to her house to make sure she made it home from her midnight shift at the hospital. She wasn't home. I called the hospital to see if she was there working late. As the receptionist got back on the phone, I was told that she was not there, and more than likely she was at breakfast with the other nurses. That was a normal thing for my mom to do. Something didn't seem right. Why would anyone be out in that miserable weather for breakfast? I followed my gut. I started back tracking the route Mom would take home from the hospital. I went on the highway just a block or so from where my Dad had his accident, but I could not continue. The roads were iced up, and my car began to slide off the highway. I gained control, but could go no further. I couldn't reach Mom on her cell phone that I gave her. Cell phones were brand new at the time, and I gave Mom one to use in case of emergency or to use if she needed it while on the roads. No answer. No one had seen Mom as I called everyone I could think of. I continued on toward the office in the opposite direction still looking. I was already late opening the office, but I didn't care. I continued my search. I finally got the call that my mother had slid off the road and was found stranded in a ditch. I found out that I was just within a few yards from reaching her on the highway where she slid off on the same ice that I had lost control of my own car with. I did not see her. Apparently, Mom was so far down you couldn't see her car. She was injured, and her glasses were knocked off. She was taken to the hospital where she worked, but thankfully not seriously injured. I called her at the hospital. I said, "Mom, I went looking for you, but I couldn't get to you on the ice. Are you ok?" Mom had hit the steering wheel and was trapped in the car. I continued, "How did anyone find you? You could have frozen to death." My mother had a strange answer. While trapped in the car in the cold and with no glasses to see, her cell phone was also knocked around. She said she heard someone on her cell phone saying "Hello, Hello?" Somehow Mom was able to find the handle of the phone. It was someone at the hospital on the other line. Apparently, the last phone call my mom made on her cell phone was to check her schedule earlier that week at the hospital a few days before. Her cell phone had redialed the last number she called as it was knocked around in the accident. Emergency personnel were able to locate her and keep her from freezing to death on the highway. It was a miracle. Yet, I knew it was something more than a miracle. Someone was trying to tell me to go find her and keep looking.

## Chapter 39 Ride and there goes twenty bucks

I always passed this car lot on my commute into the office. I saw this outstanding looking vehicle. It was white with a long nose. It looked like an old Rolls Royce. I decided to pick up Mom one day to take her along to look this car. I just wanted to take it for a test drive with no intention of buying it. She happily agreed, and off we went. When we arrived, we were greeted by an older man who owned the car lot. I said, "We would like to take that white car for a test drive, sir." Unfortunately, I did not get the response I had hoped for. He said, "I am sorry but that vehicle was sold yesterday, and I am finalizing it today with someone else." I wasn't going to take no for an answer and had to find a way to persuade him. I really wanted to test drive it. I said, "Sir, I know it is sold, but we came all this way just to take a short test drive. This is my mom here, and she is a registered nurse. I am also a business owner, and we are responsible drivers. If I leave you with the keys to my car, will you please just let us drive it down the street a couple of blocks?" He again said, "No. I am sorry, but it is sold." I began to ask him the history on the car and how he got his hands on such a gorgeous piece of machinery. He explained that it used to belong to the quarterback of the Tennessee Titans, and it ended up in an auction. He continued to tell me how he got in the car business and how he got this car. You know, just some car talk. After a while I said, "Well, it sure is a pretty car. Too bad I can't take it for a ride. Are you sure I can't just take it for a moment? My mother and I will be right back." I pulled out my car keys once again to hand to him in exchange for his keys.

Against his better judgment, he finally agreed to let Mom and I take it for a test drive. He said, "You two seem harmless enough." We hopped in and turned the key to the alluring sound of its roar and meticulously drove away in the Rolls Royce replica. It was a sweet car, and we felt like royalty in it. I did exactly what I said we would do, and we took it a few blocks down and came back to return it. Unfortunately when we got there, he had several new customers that stopped in that busy Saturday as Mom and I sat in the car. We were waiting to tell him how nice it drove and to return the keys. We waited, and waited, and waited, but he was too occupied. Being me, I decided that if he was that busy, surely he wouldn't mind if we kept the car a little longer. I drove off of the parking lot once again. This time we went everywhere with the Rolls replica, even to a local campground. We had small children running along the side of the car to see the royalty or dignitaries driving through like the president just came into town. People waved by the dozens as we passed by. We were having such a blast that I guess we forgot how long we had the replica car. By the time we realized it, we had been gone over an hour! We decided we better hurry back and return the car. The owner of the car lot came out in a panicking rush and said, "Where have you two been? I was just about to call the police that I got scammed by two ladies that stole my car!" I said, "Well…I tried to return it, but you were too busy." In a big huff, he swiftly took his keys back from me and checked the car over. Then he basically threw us off the lot. Well, we did technically have his permission. I am sure his story to the police officer that a registered nurse and a business owner just scammed him would make him look laughable. Plus he had my keys and my car in his own possession.

Mom and I laughed all day about it, and I said to my mother, "Well that was a memory not to forget, but let's not do that again in the near future." She agreed we were a little naughty. No more test driving for a while.

Momma was always up for a nice trip every once in a while. I took Momma with me on a business trip to Texas with a side trip to New Orleans. We found a nice little cafe along Bourbon Street in New Orleans and enjoyed our first real bowl of gumbo soup. It was spectacular with a French flair in some places. Other places were kind of dirty, and the streets smelled like a garbage can. I suppose it probably smelled from the festivities of the night before. Along our walks on the famously known Bourbon Street, there was a gypsy lady with Tarot cards to read your fortune. Momma wouldn't join in. She said she had a bad experience once and did not want to ever do it again. I just thought it would be something fun to do. I handed the gypsy my twenty bucks and waited for her to start placing down my cards. I remember a card with a woman and man embraced. The gypsy lady looked at me with very serious eyes and began, "I can see the man you are with, and you are married to him.........." How would she know if I was even married or not, but I was sure it was a guess on her part. It was just for fun, right? What does she know anyways? She continued, "I see this same man.........And he is laughing at you. He does love you in a strange way, a bad kind of love. I see him, and he is still laughing at you." She placed another card down with a baby in a woman's arms. She continued, "I also see a baby in your future." I guess you could say I didn't buy into her ranting and chanting. I said to myself, "Well, there goes that twenty bucks." I was hoping she would tell me I would win the lottery or something like that. She continued, "He will not be the only man you will ever love." What a joke. I was for sure being played as a fool for my money. So I walked away with twenty less dollars in my pocket and viewed it as something to do just for fun...I certainly wasn't ever going to have a different man in my life. No way. She was so wrong. I didn't believe a word she said.

## Chapter 40 The loss

There really is no other way I can put it to you, so here it goes in a nutshell. About a month and half went by after my trip to New Orleans. My career was going very well, but my marriage went up in flames like a match in a can of gasoline. I can chalk it up to you as my marriage was nothing but one big lie, so I learned on my own. I spent many years with a man I trusted, but I found that I really never knew him or who he really was after all. While on the same day I found out I was surprisingly pregnant with my son, I also discovered he was secretly engaged to another woman. That was a bad day. At the same time, I knew I had a baby to protect. Everything I knew in my life was gone. I watched him take off an engagement ring from another woman's hand that he had given her. I always said that if I ever found out that I was being cheated on, I would know exactly what I would do. This betrayal was beyond that. I would not be someone's fool. It would be over. That's was when I realized I really didn't know who I was either. Life just dealt me a dirty hand, so what was I going to do? Against everything I always told myself I would do, I was going to keep my family together and vowed to make him a better person. I was not going to fail.

I became my own fool, yet I knew I was better than that. Looking back I realized I just wasn't ready to let go of my family, not him. For a while it seemed to be what I wanted to do. As the time pressed on, that was not the case for me anymore. I could never get past his betrayals, although we stayed together with some days better than others with a handful of joys in between. I immersed myself in my work and all the children's activities sometimes just to keep distracted from the reality of my situation. I somehow detached myself from it and began to learn something new. I studied and got certified as a paralegal just for the knowledge, and it helped me tremendously in my line of work and business.

My oldest sister took me aside one day while I was still pregnant. She said, "When another door closes, another one opens." She gave me a big sister talk. It was the first one ever from her as she did her best to comfort me. She moved out when I was young with 14 years difference between us, but she was always around. I guess you could say we really never got to know one another very well up to that point. My oldest sister was the "Big Hen" in the house, but don't let her soft brown eyes and short blonde hair with a small stature fool you. She could be as tough as they come while being kind at the same time. Her siblings were her children that she helped to raise, and she chose to never have any of her own. Later in life, our long talks became very important treasure to me. Many talks made me I realized how much sacrifice it was with her always taking care of all 7 siblings, something I never experienced being the youngest in the family. She once gave me a very special pin to wear and a bracelet as a symbol of our sisterhood with love. I got to see the softer side of her. She could be hard on you and tell it like it is. One thing was for sure, she would always come to anyone's rescue any time or any day. She came to mine. I loved her so much for that, but I wasn't ready to open any new doors. I knew I had to walk through each and every door by myself.

My Life Single For Eight Hours

## Chapter 41 I know where I was during 9-11

During the time of the reconciliation of my marriage, my son was now almost 13 months old. I was at the office one day, and suddenly the room began to spin. Then the next thing I remember was everything sounded like Chinese, and I could not understand anything. I began to have seizures. The only way to describe it to you is a numbing and tingling sensation that becomes a volcano right before eruption. It begins at your toes to your head, and then all that you hear is white noise. I was young and healthy, so what could it be?

I remember the morning of September 11th. I was supposed to be on airplane out of Chicago to fly and get care at the Mayo Clinic in Minnesota that morning. As fate would have it, my seizures were so severe that I could not make that flight. Instead we were to drive to Minnesota to get my complete evaluation and diagnosis of what I had. I was watching television and the morning news waiting for our rental car to be delivered shortly. It was all planned out that relatives would keep the children while we traveled. As I was watching the breaking news, I watched in horror in real time as both planes hit the towers. The rental car pulled up and my bags were packed to go. I had to make a heart wrenching decision to stay or go, not knowing what was to unfold in our country that morning. I had to leave my children or stay. I knew I had to get well for my children. The heartbreaking decision was made that I would continue on to the Mayo Clinic. In the back of my mind the whole time, I wasn't sure if I would ever see my children again after hugging and kissing them goodbye.

My heart was just torn apart. We drove around Chicago, which was eerily still and quiet. Everyone hunkered down in their homes afraid. I only saw five cars the entire trip to Minnesota that day. Chicago stood lifeless like a still picture.

After arriving, I was admitted to the hospital with test after test while one of the worst events was still unfolding in our country. People were still sick during 9-11, and doctors pressed on to do their job. They were true heroes that day. I recall being given a cognitive test on a simple sheet of paper with some basic math equations to complete. 6 x 8. I did not know the answer. I began to realize that I didn't know how to multiply number anymore, and I became very afraid. I didn't even remember how to even start to multiply them. I had lost part of my cognitive ability due to the seizures. Finally after days, they released me and would forward their final findings to my family doctor and an oncologist of my choice.  As it was explained, I had some sort of blood disorder. Yet, they would not be specific and told me to go over the results with an oncologist as the final report would be forwarded.

I met with the oncologist back home.  As he entered the evaluation room with Momma by my side, the doctor turned pale as a ghost. He asked me if I knew why I was there. I gestured with a nod and said, "Yes, I have some sort of blood disorder or discrepancy." He began, "You have a form of Leukemia, and your blood count is high.  A very aggressive form." He then explained that I had to have a biopsy of my bone marrow to determine what exactly we were dealing with. With Mom a nurse, I valued her input and support. It was agreed that a biopsy of my bone marrow would be performed that very day. With my mother and two other nurses holding me down on a table, he drilled into my hip. I was wide awake with no pain medication or it would alter the test. Screaming in excruciating pain, I was held down so the tool he was drilling into my hip could collect the specimen. My mother had tears, and I knew it was serious.

The months pressed on along with the seizures, and it was determined that the Leukemia included my white blood cells to be elevated. So for the next year, I took test after test, hospital visits after doctor visits, and try after try.

With nothing left to lose, Momma finally took me to a holistic expert for alternatives to modern medicine and got me on herbal medicine. I became a regular buying special remedies with this herbal specialist. They began a series of tests of my hair and urine to evaluate what was going on. It was to basically reset my blood cells and clean them out by using nontraditional medicine. Momma was so patient with me. She even got index cards and flash cards with numbers, and together she taught me how to multiply numbers again. Without Momma, I would have not recovered. My immune system was a mess. She worked on every aspect of my care while trying to come up with different types of holistic remedies she swore by, just like when I was burned as a child. Eventually, I made outstanding strides. Almost a full recovery, but not quite, but almost. The seizures had subsided for the time being. To this day, my white blood count runs high, and I am monitored and prone to infections.

My Life Single For Eight Hours

## Chapter 42 The Final Quiz

I was finally in a better place in my life as far as my health was concerned, but my marriage still was not. Then it happened one day when a man came to my office looking for a donation. I gave him my donation, and he began to leave. Then he came back to my desk. Thinking that I hadn't given him enough, I waited to hear his sales pitch for more money. I always donated, but this guy wouldn't leave. He stood there and looked at me as he said, "Many people have wronged you in your life. I can see that." Although there was some truth to what he said, I felt it was vague and anyone could say that. I politely listened, because what does he know about me anyways, right? It got stranger. He told me that I had two angels that protected me. One in the front of me, and one in the back of me. Then he told me that I was very loved. He politely and softly said to me, "I know you are loved. When I leave here, I will prove it all to you." Then I just turned my back to him to distance myself away and had enough of his sales pitch. As I turned back around to make sure he was finally gone, I saw that he had left…Never to be seen again. I said to myself, "Well, that had to be the strangest person I ever met in my life. What was that all about?" I was actually so glad he was gone. Shaking it off, suddenly the phone rang. It was Momma calling. She said, "You won't believe what happened at work last night in the hospital." I exclaimed, "What?" She said, "You know I have no time to myself and not even a break during my shift, but I just had a moment to myself at the hospital. I was flipping through this travel magazine at work, and I came across a picture of that shark sculpture in the roof." With both of us excited to talk further, she explained that she tore out the colored photo and put into in her pocket. We agreed that when I got home from the office that she would meet me there to give it to me. I then told her about the strange encounter I had at the office right before she called. Now I hadn't looked at my art portfolio for a long time, years even. I found it in the closet at home and dusted it off. I unzipped the case, and I found the newspaper article I collected in art class when I was in England. Anxiously awaiting for her arrival, I finally saw her pull in. She handed me the folded up photo from the travel magazine in her pocket. Sure enough the sculpture was the same. She said, "You know I always remember you talking about this sculpture as a child. You were obsessed with it." And I replied, "Dad promised we would see it together." Then she said, "I know, honey. I remember you saying that a lot, too." As the evening moved on, she left and the kids were fast asleep. I finally had a moment to reminisce about the day. I took out the old article from art class while attending college in Oxford, England and realized that I had never read the entire thing. I began to finally read the old newspaper article for the first time in my hands after all those years. It was then that I realized something very strange about that article. I wanted to know the facts. What are the facts you may be asking? As I read the newspaper clipping closely for the first time, I learned it was about six year dispute, and the city council of Oxford wanted the shark sculpture torn down because they felt that it was way too much of a traffic distraction and devalued properties. In the end, the property owner won. As I read further, the sculpture was erected in the roof in 1986. I read it again and again…The sculpture was in existence only in 1986.

How could that possibly be? That simply couldn't be true. There was no way it could be possible. I remembered I was in high school in 1986, so the shark sculpture could not have existed when I was a little girl. How did I know about it and obsess over it as a child? Then, and only then, I knew that the memory of when my dad and I first saw the photo of shark sculpture with his promise to see it together was a dream. Only a vivid dream, a premonition I had as a child............

Then the man that visited my office earlier that day came to mind, and I remembered what he had said. He told me that he would prove to me that I was loved, and prove that I had two angels that protected me. One in the front, and one in the back of me.

My premonition of my dad and I when I was a child had suddenly become reality. I knew how much Dad loved me. I couldn't tell you who the protector was that stood behind me. I just knew right then that Dad was the one that stood in front of me the entire time protecting me from danger since he died, just as he did when he was alive. You see, Dad died in his car accident earlier that same year shortly before the shark sculpture was erected in 1986. In some divine way, Dad stood with me that day in England to see the shark sculpture together...just like he had promised me in my vivid childhood dream...And Dad always kept his promises...........Then he gave me one final quiz to figure it all out.

It was proven to me that day that there are things in life that are simply unexplainable that truly have an existence, even against all my logical, clear, and factual thinking.

## Chapter 43 She called to say she slept with Jesus

During the constant turbulence in my married life, I still made time for one particular sister who always stood up for me as young child. She was also the sister I took quarters from out her tip jar when I was young. Let me tell you, she was the life of the party and could work a room like you have never seen before. She took me to my first bar when I was just 16 and got me a fake ID to get in. I got to see firsthand how she worked her magic, and I witnessed people, both men and women, become absolutely entranced with her and came under her spell. Free drinks and food all night, anything we wanted. She was just exhilarating and electrified the room! She always reminded me of a version of the cartoon character Betty Boop with big brown eyes and short brown hair. Yes, she was always my Betty Boop with her cute laugh to match.

My sister had her challenges throughout the years, just like anyone else. I always told my staff in the office that if she called no matter what I was doing, I would take that call. Most of the time, it was just general conversation or to relay a message to Mom for her when she couldn't get a hold of her. Something changed well into my adulthood with my sister, and her bubbly sparkle was no longer there. Anytime she called, I would be there for her. She called one day, and I had the call immediately transferred to me.

Here is how the conversation went...It was not the usual tone in her voice I was used to hearing. This time she had more excitement than usual. She exclaimed over the phone, "I slept with Jesus!"

I quickly closed my office blinds and closed my door. I knew in an instant something was very, very wrong. So I repeated back to her what she said in the form of a question, "You slept with Jesus?" She questioned me why I didn't ask how it went...I was trying to figure out how to tell my sister that it wasn't true, again without upsetting her. I continued to let her tell me the story. She began by saying, "Well, at first the intimacy was great, but then it got really weird." I replied, "Image that...Weird how?" She replied, "It was really nice at first, but then it just got stranger and stranger. I accidentally called him the wrong name." I questioned, "The wrong name?" She began to continue, "Well, when he touched me while we were in bed together, it felt so good that I accidentally yelled out oh my God, oh my God. I called him the wrong name and called him God and not Jesus!"

"Sister," I said gently, "you did not sleep with Jesus." She adamantly replied, "YES I DID!!!" Then she began to explain. Come to find out Jesus was a nickname of a local man that she met when she was at a Halloween party, and they ended up spending the night together. We both began to laugh for a moment at the confusion, and for me, it was a sigh of relief. My sister was perfectly fine. She wanted to tell me that she was so happy to have a human touch, an intimate evening, and some tenderness...Something she hadn't had in quite some time. She had her immaculate sparkle back, and the vivacious sister I knew was back, too. Yes, my little Betty Boop was back.

My sister became a blanket of comfort to me no matter what she had going on in her life. Sometimes, I just needed to hear her cute little laugh which made my day. She told me when Mom and Dad first came home with the twins, she picked me to take care of. I called her sometimes and played her a favorite jovial song I picked just for her, even though I was a terrible singer. She would just sing along as I sang it to her, and we just giggled together. She was my immense source of laughter, even in my darkest days. She gave me a turquoise ring to wear, and called it our sister ring. She had always been very loyal and loving to me throughout my life since day one. She will never know how much all that meant to me. I sent her a sister blanket to wrap up with as a source of my comfort at all times, just incase...

By learning from my sister, I soon realized there was a fine line from being a vivacious woman that loved life to how quickly the pressures of life could attempt to take the vibrant spirit away from someone who was always so kind to me...In that moment, I needed to somehow make peace with the bad things that happened in my life by the people who wronged me before it destroyed me...and I wasn't about to let that happen to me.

My Life Single For Eight Hours

## Chapter 44 The Biggest Fall yet

Some details in my book are harder and more painful to write than others, but I want to be candid with anyone reading and share my genuine story. Please allow me to share with you some of my deepest pain that I went through. My marriage was at a boiling point of no return. I filed for a divorce and the life I knew ended, too. I eventually had to walk away from it all. I lost most of my possessions, houses, and eventually my businesses. You name it. The one thing for sure was I still had my children. I agreed to joint custody and I never asked for child support. It couldn't be left at that. As detrimental as it was, eventually my rights were taken away from me, too. With no money left to fight another court battle to defend my custody, I was once again drug into court to be told what an unfit mother I was, and that I was in financial ruins. I was being punished for what? Interesting enough for all those years the times I took them to the doctors, all the times I cared for them, consoled them when there was a bad storm, and read short stories to them meant not a damn thing in the courts...Nor did his betrayals. With no money left to defend myself, I still fought back fiercely. I turned both the judge and lawyer in to the Judiciary Commission to investigate the court. Although the Judiciary Commission's purpose was to investigate extensively, the Commission was not allowed to change any judge's ruling, regardless of their findings. So there I was without custody of my children, one of the lowest points in my life. I got to be with my children every other weekend, birthdays, holidays, and other occasions.

148

While some used the court's decision as a permit to unleash their cruelty and unkindness to me, others used it as a center of gossip and ridicule. Anyone and everyone who wanted to join in on the pleasure to watch a successful woman fall rapidly while losing everything did so with pure evilness. Others were simply just cruel in nature. As I was constantly defending myself as a mother, I was the target of dirty looks, shaming, and a witch hunt. All I wanted to do was be a mom. They never knew me for who I really was. Like I said, life can change in an instant. To anyone here reading my book, maybe you have had a similar experience from oppressing adults, or maybe you are an adult doing the persecuting or out for revenge...Stop to think for a minute. One day children grow up, and they are smarter than you think they are. They know the truth and know the person you always will be toward them. I accepted the court's decision as only a useless piece of paper to me, and not the true love I had for my children, and no one could ever take that away from me...ever.

## Chapter 45 My dedicated chapter

Mom and Dad always said if you don't have anything nice to say about someone, don't say it at all.

I dedicate this chapter to those who have ever wronged me in my life ............ (silence).

I don't even have to say a single word...It is already written in the dictionary for them. Just look it up.

As painful as this may sound, I thank the ones who have wronged me. I have made my peace with it, but I was not destroyed. It just brought out more strength in me for my future battles in life to come.

My Life Single For Eight Hours

## Chapter 46 Single for eight hours

The final divorce papers were ready for me to sign. I read the divorce papers over one last time, and then I signed the document just as I had always signed my name on any old document. It was filed. I was so done. It became final, and I could close that door in my life forever. I was divorced. I guess you could say that same evening I just wanted to get out and get some fresh air to forget about the day's events.

About a week or so before my divorce, we met on the computer one random day. I sent him a crappy message, and I was not very nice about it. Who is this person I am talking about? Read further and soon you will find out. That's how it all started out anyways...Somehow it didn't backfire on me, not like it should have. It actually made him curious, and he found me to be a bit sassy. I further said, "Look, I am not some toothless old lady talking to you." He responded by asking for a picture to prove it, and then he would know for sure who he was talking to. I sent him a picture. I was always a private person. I didn't dare discuss my life or details of my divorce to him. He only knew I was getting a divorce. Not specifics anyways. We had been talking on the phone throughout the past few days. He asked me out on a date. A date? I have to be honest, I had put off having a date with him and scheduled one for a few weeks later. He sounded disappointed and said, "A couple of weeks?" I put off the date just in case I wanted to back out.

After I signed my divorce papers, I called him on the phone that day and asked him what he was doing. I had changed my mind and wanted to move our date forward to that very night. He happily agreed. My divorce papers were signed only a few hours ago, but I had my first date with the time set in place…Thus, I was single for eight hours when we met for the first time face to face for my very first date. I entered into this date with the attitude, "Ok, let's see where this goes." If anything, I was out for the very first time after my divorce with absolutely no expectations at all. None. I just really wanted some good conversation and a nice evening to forget about the events of the day. No pressure.

I was running late (not a good way to start) trying to get ready for the evening. I called him on the way to tell him I was going to be about 20 minutes late, and our date actually began on the telephone until I arrived. Shortly before I arrived, we hung up the phone. I drove around the last corner, and I saw him standing there for the first time. As I parked, I couldn't stop looking at him from a distance while I sat inside of my car. I tried to gather my thoughts as I began to get confused. Very confused actually…

They say that there is such a thing called love at first sight. I said that is a bunch of hogwash or rubbish, depending on what side of the world you were on. Please, whatever. It was a myth, nonsense, and a bunch of garbage. I was a logical person…so you couldn't even try to convince me of its existence. My firm stance in life has always been if something truly exists, then prove it to me or prove me wrong.

I couldn't stop having this overwhelming feeling come over me. I was losing my composure very quickly as I turned the corner in my car and saw him for the first time. My mind was racing…My heart was pounding as he approached my vehicle to greet me. "Hurry up and get it together, girl," I said to myself. I didn't know what exactly was happening to me, let alone understand it. After all, I was single for only eight hours. There was no logic to the whole situation I was in. All I can tell you is that when I saw him for the very first time, I had instantly fallen in love with him. Yep, I proved myself wrong. I pondered the questions, "How can this be happening? What is this?" It felt like a pickup truck had hit me hard, like slamming into a wall, and now I have to keep this to myself? I only had a few seconds to gain my composure and to be careful not expose myself to what was going on. Can you imagine? I opened the car door as he stood there to greet me. He smelled so good and looked so nicely dressed. Oh, now that made it even harder the closer I got to him. I stood up to get out, and we were face to face for the first time. I was in a panic. I had to gather myself and keep my secret ......that I was in love with him. That wasn't part of my plan. WHAT??? So much for no pressure.

I was greeted with a sultry hello, and responded with a soft hello back to him. Then before I knew what happened, he reached from behind his back and pulled something out to hand to me that he had been hiding. It was a bouquet of six red roses. Stunned, I politely accepted the delightful roses and nearly fainted, I tell you. I thought, "What a sweet thing to do. Roses for me, little ole me?" For a moment, a peaceful feeling came over me. I knew at that moment that I would be ok. I mean I didn't want to blow it. We walked into the coffee shop, and he ordered us two hot chocolates.  As he walked to the counter, I continued to secretly gaze at the man that I was in love with. It made no sense. It gave me a moment from a distance to completely look at him and again try to logically explain to myself all the reasons it was not happening. I could not come up with anything. I was mesmerized when he walked back to the table where I was sitting. I began to take my jacket off. He quickly jumped up to remove my jacket for me, and I was a wreck all over again. The more polite gestures he offered, the more of a hot mess I became.

We walked out of the shop and down the street to a club he knew of. He reached out and held my hand for the first time. I remember how warm his hand was and how gently he held mine. When he touched my hand for the first time, it was the most stunning moment of my life. Something I hadn't had for a very long time, and it felt so damn good. As we walked into the club with roses in my hand, we were greeted by a woman who stopped dead in her tracks when she saw him. Then she looked at me and said, "I don't know where you found him, but you better keep him." I said to myself sarcastically and being in total denial, "Ok, I am being set up. How much did he pay her to say that?" I began to tell myself crap like that just doesn't happen out of the blue trying to convince myself the whole date thing was a farce. I responded simply with, "Well, this is just our first date." Again she repeated herself by saying, "I don't know how or where you met him, but you better keep him." Did she think I was stupid?

Puzzled, I gave him one last suspicious gaze as we went into the basement of the club where there was a nice couch, coffee area, and a bar. My guard was suddenly on high alert,

My Life Single For Eight Hours

and I became somewhat conflicted. He began by telling me that the young girl we just met was the bartender there, and that she had served him. They would have conversations about how he was getting divorced. She would be a source of information on how the dating world worked and what girls liked, which was a new territory for him. He then revealed to me that I was his first date. I eventually put my guard back down, and he quickly broke through my barriers. I had to criticize myself to have thought I was being set up, and he paid her to say that. She already knew what a great guy he was through their conversations...and he really was a great guy. All in all, this first date was new territory to me and to him. I have to admit, I let him do most of the talking. I really was fearful he would find out my secret that I had fallen in love with him, even though my attempts to deny it failed miserably. I was absolutely petrified that I would be revealed. He really worked very hard to make sure our date was perfect. I felt I needed to give him a small break from all of his hard work and to just come back being myself without terror of this secret. I strategically excused myself and went to the ladies room. When I walked back out, I saw him in the chair just sitting there patiently waiting for my return. Again, this overwhelming feeling came over me. I don't know why, but I walked straight up to him and without saying anything, I gave him a kiss on the lips. After that, it became kiss after kiss. The best thing was he kissed me back! I was hooked, and so was he.

The next day he called me as promised, and over the phone he asked me something I will never forget. He asked me on the phone to be his girlfriend. Can you believe it? That was so unexpected. Unfortunately, I did not respond with a favorable answer. I was just divorced the day before, not to mention all the heartache I had been through. I was not ready to just jump into something. I responded with, "I just got divorced yesterday. I am not sure." I did not give him a straight answer. Then he responded with, "I will win your heart. I will." I said to myself, "He doesn't know where my heart has been." He repeated the question one more time very sweetly, "Will you be my girlfriend?" It was in that instant that I knew he had already won my heart from the very beginning. I responded again with a more favorable answer by saying, "Yes, I would love to be your girlfriend." I couldn't fight off my feelings for him anymore, and I surrendered to fact that I was in love with him. I didn't dare tell him that though...No way! I didn't want to scare the guy off and make him think I was some sort of eccentric woman with bizarre ideas. Wouldn't you think the same thing? I was beginning to think the whole thing was insane. As we hung up the phone, I realized my life was about to change...And so it did. As we began dating, it was obvious that things moved very quickly. Too fast for my family that watched out for me. They had not ever experienced in their life what I just did, love at first sight.

We just clicked with no logical explanation to our natural bond. We shared many long talks just about anything and everything, except for my one big secret. Then it happened. I finally told him the truth one day. I explained that I had fallen in love with him the first time I ever saw him. I was going to get it off my chest and waited to see what he had to say about that. I expected to hear, "That's crazy, just plain nonsense." Instead he told me something I never expected. He had a mysterious confession to reveal to me as well. He had fallen in love with me the first time he saw me when I opened the car door. He described how my long blonde hair had had fallen to the side of my face as I opened the car door and stood next to him. In that instant, he knew he was madly in love with me. We both just couldn't explain any of it. It was real, love at first sight, that's for sure. While I was sitting and writing this book, he expressed to me that he believed we were put together not by our own choice, but part of something we will never be able to explain...That it was meant to happen. We just had to meet somehow.

Our relationship took off like the blazes of a wildfire. It was less than a month after our first date when he came by one afternoon, and I was in the house cleaning the dining room. He reached in his pocket intuitively and pulled out a ring box. That was just his way, instinctive and always by surprise. He asked me to marry him, and just like that put the ring on my finger. Of course I said yes. Hell yes..!!! I told him that there was a catch though. As tradition, he would have to ask for my momma's blessing.

My Life Single For Eight Hours

## Chapter 47 Only make the gravy

We had been together less than a month. Christmas was at my mom's house. All siblings, children, nieces, nephews, sister-in-laws, and brother-in-laws came to gather. It was always a huge crowd at Mom's house. She always made it a very special occasion, and I was going to bring my fiancé to Christmas. I had not told anyone that he had given me a ring, and they hadn't even met him yet. As I walked in with him, the whispers started in my ear. The family's murmurs began, "He has a sexy accent. He is so cute. He's so tall, and he smells really good." As he did with every event in his life, he took the bulls by the horn with confidence and made his way through the crowd of family members. I graciously introduced him to everyone. They welcomed him with cheer and some skepticism, I have to admit.

The time came that my children would be off for Christmas with their father's family. I had to leave my fiancé alone with my family for about 20 minutes to go drop off my four children. My mom stopped me at the door to remind me that I had to make the gravy when I got back. Well, as great as he was, he stepped right in and said he would make the gravy for me. I told Mom, "Yes, of course. He is a great cook." So Mom agreed. While she got the potatoes off the stove, she would make the mashed potatoes while he made the gravy. It was a done deal.

I returned from dropping the kids off, and it was eerily quiet in the house. Not the usual hustle and bustle of the normal Christmas gatherings I experienced my whole life. In an instant, I knew something was wrong. What could possibly go wrong in 20 minutes? I pulled him aside. I said, "What happened? What did you do?" He simply replied, "Oh nothing. As I was making the gravy next to your mom in the kitchen, I asked her for her blessing to marry you." I was shaking in my shoes and almost passed out…He was to meet my family and nothing more! I replied, "What? Now? How?" He simply replied, "Well, I thought it would be a good time to ask your mom to marry you. Everyone was together and having such a great time." That was just his way, direct and to the point. My mother looked at me as I approached the kitchen area where she was finishing the mashed potatoes. She said to both of us trying to be neutral and staying true to her calm nature, "Well, if you kids know what you are doing…," and she finished stirring the potatoes. It was out in the open. Now we were the center of attention and the talk of the entire Christmas gathering. One relative politely pulled him aside after dinner to say what was on his mind emphasizing, "She is vulnerable." He didn't agree with the engagement at all. My fiancé simply replied to the opposition that he just loved me, and he did it with class and dignity defending our engagement. I was proud of him, and knew I was with a man that could hold his own. After a while, the entire family got back to the celebrations of that Christmas Day as usual. It was definitely a Christmas to remember…gravy and all.

Now being a mother myself, I have to admit if my child came home and knew someone less than a month and got engaged shortly after, I would not be very enthusiastic and naturally concerned. It is just an instinct. To my mother's and family's defense, they just were looking out for me.

My mom spent the next couple of years giving me the snake eyes with two fingers pointed to her eye and then back at me to let me know she was watching him. Jokingly, I would snake eye her right back and say, "I know, Momma, but he's a good man." She would always simply reply with a little smirk, "I am still watching him. You're my baby."

.

My Life Single For Eight Hours

## Chapter 48 There's no getting it out of me

Now I was engaged and with Momma's blessing. My fiancé
was not the type to pry into my past. He never asked anything
about it and never pressured me with any deep questions
until this one night. We sat at the end of the bed after a long
day at work. He said, "I need to ask you something." He
began, "Why did you get a divorce and what happened?" I
was a private person, and wasn't going to let anyone get the
details out of me. They were buried pretty deep. I always just
worked through my problems and kept going. Honestly, no
one ever asked me that question before, nor did I ever give
them the chance to. He continued softly, "I really would like
to know." I wasn't ready to share any details of my pain and
never trusted anyone with them enough to talk about it. I felt
that I could keep that to myself and just deal with it. I just
wanted him to love me for who I was, and not because of
bad things that happened to me. He did love me very deeply
though, and I felt he should know. At the same time I didn't
want to reveal my failures in life, at least that's the way I
looked at things. He softly begins, "Just tell me." So that
evening for the first time, I told him what had happened to
me. I trusted him with my undeniable pain, and in return he
never judged me. He just put his arms around me to let me
weep for the first time. He kissed the top of my head and
tenderly said, "It's all right, baby doll. It's all right."

That conversation made me realize how much trust we had between us. He loved me for who I was, not because of my pain. I trusted him with my life from there on out, and he trusted me with his.

## Chapter 49 What really happens in a restroom

Now before I get into this, when we met I was divorced, and he was almost at the end of the process of his own a divorce that was filed. We had planned our wedding a few months later. We met with the pastor three times and had to discuss our relationship and get his blessing to proceed with a ceremony. It was a charming church with a bronze organ and cathedral ceilings, but there was a problem. A huge one...

Since his divorce was not contested, all that had to happen was the judge had sign the final papers, and it wasn't done yet. The wedding was getting closer and closer, and the judge still had not signed any of the paperwork even after all these months. Believing it was signed off, my fiancé went to the courts to find out why papers had not been signed by the judge. There was no reason for the delay. We were down to the last wire before our wedding. What was going on? Come to find out there was a huge case going on, and that judge presided over it. The big case was closed to the public. The judge was not signing any papers and was totally consumed with this huge case. He was behind with signing documents. My fiancé met me at my office to describe what was going on. We couldn't get married because the judge had not signed off on the final paperwork for months and was backed up. We decided we would have to cancel the wedding.

The next morning, I was bound and determined to have that wedding. I came up with a plan. I would go to the courts and get it done no matter what. I mean all the judge had to do was sign the document, right? I called my fiancé and told him that I would get something done. He was not on board with the idea as he had already tried. Well, I guess he found another side of me that day.

That morning, I implemented my plan. I went to the courthouse knowing that this huge case was going on and that judge would be sitting in the courtroom during the proceedings. Since it was a closed case to the public, there was a desk and a woman sitting next to the double doors of the courtroom. She was there to make sure no one could get in. I approached her in my business suit and briefcase. I strategically asked if I could enter the hearing as I was a certified paralegal and wanted to learn from the case. It was up to her to decide to let me in or not. To my amazement, my persuasion worked! I was allowed in. I slowly opened these double doors to the courtroom as an attorney was drilling a police officer on the witness stand. The moment I walked in, the attorney suddenly stopped in his tracks. Startled, he stared at me as the courtroom full of people shifted toward me when I walked in. The attorney actually lost his place while hammering this police officer. I am sure he thought I was a surprise witness or something to the case, and he was floored that I had just walked in. I walked straight through the rows of people and sat myself in the second row. On the corner seat, I was a woman on a mission and was going to get that paper signed.

It was right before noon as I entered the courtroom. I had already found where the nearest ladies restroom was (very important). I began to scan the room picking out the people in my view. I zoned in on who was the court reporter, who was the judge's secretary, and another lady of importance to the judge. I knew that at noon that they must be taking a lunch break from the case, and as a woman, I also knew those ladies would be heading straight for the bathroom. Sure as it was, the judge dismissed for recess. I quickly made my way to the ladies restroom to wash my hands before anyone else entered. Just as I had planned! The three women I watched closely came into the restroom staring me down as I washed my hands. I said to the one of them, "Wow, that is some case in there." One replied baffled, "Yes, indeed it is. We were all wondering who you are. Who are you?" I replied, "Well, I am not really here for the case, and I am not a witness." They looked even more bewildered. I said, "I am here because I need your help, and I am looking for a miracle. I have a wedding planned and my fiancé needs the judge to sign his final divorce papers so we can get married. I thought maybe you ladies could be so kind and help me to get the judge to sign those papers." They all looked at each other wide eyed and one said, "That is the most romantic thing I have ever heard! Of course we will help!" The restroom was buzzing with excitement among all of us, and together we became women on a mission to get it done. Soon phone calls and conversations were made as they pulled together to make it happen. Guess what? I walked out with divorce papers signed. It was official. I never saw those women again, but often I think back to the gratitude and respect I had for them and that bonding moment.

Without telling my fiancé the events of the day, I asked him to meet me back at the office. He walked in with a look of disappointment on his face. I handed him the folder from across my desk and said, "My darling, here are your papers." To his astonishment, he couldn't believe what I just handed him. I got it done. I told him the whole story. In an instant, we picked up where we left off planning the wedding.

My Life Single For Eight Hours

I said to him, "Sometimes in life you just have to be a little creative."

For those of you who have ever wondered what really happens in the ladies restroom, my answer to that is this…Now you know.

## Chapter 50 The big night

Every woman and man consummates their marriage with their first night together as husband and wife. I would love to share all of the juicy details with you. So here it goes...........

My fiancé made the event perfect. My sister, The Great Chef, had a horse ranch and brought a white carriage drawn by a white horse and parked it outside of the church. My children joyfully threw rice and were part of the entire celebration as we boarded the carriage. We were paraded through town by the white horse as we celebrated our commitment to each other. The reception was at my house, and we had everything donated. My talented uncle, Mom's brother, played the guitar and sang songs with delightful music. We had a hog roast grilled outside as a wedding gift by the same sister that brought the white horse. Her ranch hands cooked the hog from the break of dawn. Everyone brought side dishes of delicious variety. What a valiant effort from my family and friends to bring together the most fabulous day. Not your traditional reception by any means, but then again nothing about my relationship was traditional either. It simply was an unforgettable evening.

We had our first dance together as husband and wife, and we swayed gently to the music totally in love. The house was full of people as the celebration went late into the night. Music, dancing, laughter, and reminiscing were plentiful...Then an old video surfaced of me as a wedding gift. Let's play the video. My loyal friends and hog wrestling partners from the county fair were there to celebrate with me.

Finding out what it was, it happened to be an old video of me hog wrestling in the mud chasing a full grown hog, lifting it up, and putting it into a tire. It was the championship video. Just as the video was playing with my old hog wrestling partners and close friends, my newly wedded husband stopped to see what the laughter and cheering was all about. Well, that's when he found out his wife was a hog wresting champion. I joking said "Honey, I guess I never told you that part about me." He was in total shock, but it was priceless...

As the cold winter night pressed on during our wedding reception, so did a storm. An ice storm rolled in and below zero weather set in. A pipe had come apart, and my basement was flooded during the reception. My two oldest brothers trampled though the water to shut it off and repair it. I felt pretty bad Big Brother's cell phone fell in the water. That is what big brothers just do. By now, half of the guests had made the decision to try to get home during the storm. Some traveling from far away. Unfortunately, half of my other guests were stranded at my house. In light of the situation, there was plenty to eat and extra room to sleep in. To conclude, on our wedding night half of my wedding guests stayed all night with us. We all stayed up most of the evening together, some of it waiting to get word back that the others had made it home safely. Exhausted and tired, my husband and I just fell asleep still in our reception clothing until the next morning. Oh well, again some things in life just happen. Not the wedding night you anticipated to read about...Then again, what does go as planned, right? Actually, my wedding night was wonderful and simply unforgettable.

## Chapter 51 What more could I ask for?

My husband is a full of stories from his days back in Europe of driving to the glorious mountains in Switzerland, going on the Autobahn where there is no speed limit, racing his car he built on the Nürburgring race track in Germany, and touring the islands off of Spain. He was a world traveler. One thing I must say about him was his love of cars in which we both had a passion for. Our wedding cake was even a race car and another cake with a more traditional style beautifully made by a dear friend of mine. Our shared passion for racing and vintage vehicles bonded us to the next exciting road course race or car show. Sometimes women go along to something perhaps they are not into. That was certainly not the case with me. I am right there enjoying the excitement probably as much, if not more, than he at times. Tinkering in the garage is where you will always find him. I am sometimes right along with him, enjoying getting into a little elbow grease from time to time by handing him a tool. I call him Mr. MacGyver as there is not much he can't fix. He is highly intelligent. There probably isn't any subject he can't teach me something new about, and you know how much I love to learn.

Sometimes, I ask him something simple like how our new microwave works. Instead of the basics, I get an answer like Einstein about molecules and how rays work. If it's broken, he can fix it. If it is hard to figure out, he will find a way. His passion for the technology fits right in with my curiosity about it as well. His firm attitude is "Let's get something done."

Aside from all of that, his biggest passion is our marriage and takes our vows very seriously. What more could you ask for in a guy? Honestly, you couldn't ask for a more loyal and dedicated husband. I am just so thankful he came into my life. One of the best things in life is having the unexpected just suddenly appear. He certainly changed my life.

## Chapter 52 Surviving with so little knowledge

My husband and I are really excited when we can attend a new car show. Stories of him on the German Autobahn and racing his car on the Nürburgring track in Europe were always hot topics. I just loved speed and cars. The latest cars and old vintage cars became our passion together. Before GPS, I would always have a map printed out of the event with directions as we would take off to a show. The Taste of Chicago was coming up I read somewhere, and I quickly told him I would love to go and could get all the details for him. He agreed, and we soon found ourselves planning a weekend day in Chicago. They were even going to have a car show from what I read. The weekend finally arrived, and off we went to the Taste of Chicago. The map took us on a route off the beaten path, but that was ok. I told my husband we can go past the old steel mills on Lake Michigan along the way. We came to the steel mills all vacant with a few stack pipes still smoking. It was miles long. He was fascinated with the steel mills and the history of the men that built such a great marvel to produce steel. I explained how the steel mills used the water from Lake Michigan to cool the steel. As I am reading the map, I had never remembered going to Chicago that way. I assured him we would be there soon. He kept driving. Soon we would arrive. As we passed dilapidated buildings and bars on the windows, he pulled off in a safe spot and said, "Give me that map." I quickly found the map in the backseat that I always used when traveling from state to state. He studied the one that I printed out from the internet, and I studied the one from the book. He said, "This is not Chicago! What did you do?" When I finally had both maps in my hand to compare together, my map from the internet was actually directions to East Chicago, Indiana an area known as East Chicago and West Gary. We were still in Indiana, not Illinois. He exclaimed, "My girl, how do you survive with so little knowledge?" I simply shrugged my shoulders and with a childish smile as I replied, "Gee, I don't know." With my very innocent reply, we both just busted out laughing. Yes, we were in the area known as East Chicago and West Gary, and it could be a dangerous place and a rough area at times. I mapped out directions for the festival called the Taste of East Chicago in the state of Indiana which bordered the west side of Gary and not the Taste of Chicago in Illinois. We weren't even in the correct state, and Chicago, Illinois was still about 40 minutes away. As he tried to start the car and turn the key, he said, "We need to get out of here now!" I quickly replied, "Hold on just a minute." I looked him dead in the eyes and firmly put my hand on his wrist and said, "Do you trust me?" He replied, "I trusted you with the map and look where that got us, Gary, Indiana!!!" I again looked directly at him with an idea as I repeated, "Do ..you ..trust ..me..?" We will be fine. It's an adventure, so trust me. I know that the people will not harm us, especially if there is a celebration and a good barbecue going on. They love to celebrate." I threw the maps in the backseat and disregarded them as they flew through the air. I was ready to go for an adventure. I said, "Who needs maps anyways? Life is an adventure!"

Reluctantly, he agreed and placed his wallet in his front pocket. We drove out of the west side of Gary and soon found a parking spot next to a house with bars on the windows all boarded up close to the festivities in heart of

East Chicago just a few minutes away from Gary. He locked the car doors and actually gave our car a little pat. Then he kissed the car like he was saying goodbye forever. We walked across the street to the festivities at The Taste of East Chicago. We stood out all right, definitely out of towners with my husband's accent and all. But just as I said it would happen, we were greeted with cheer and joy. We were urged to join in and welcomed with open arms. The first person to welcome us was a retired Gary police officer who was setting up the stage for music. With a smile, he directed us over to the barbecues that were going on and told us to get ourselves a bite to eat. The barbecue pits were made from old metal barrels cut in half with makeshift hinges on them. They had barbecued ribs and chicken smoldering, and the whole sky was filled with simmering smoke and a delicious aroma. We were handed a plate and a cup of ice cold cool aid. The master chef was joyfully singing as he cooked. Then they piled our plates with nothing but best of The Taste of East Chicago. Umm, ummmmmmm! It was like a masterpiece of nothing but goodness, I tell you. There was nothing like it. The music began to play and the vibes of The Taste of East Chicago, Indiana turned into one big party. After we ate, we went to the nice booths that were set up with vendors. Soon we were approached by a man with gold teeth and a dozen or more watches on his arm. While pulling up his sleeve, he asked us if we wanted to buy one. We politely declined and continued our way through the vendor booths. I have to admit, I admired his side hustle. We soon found ourselves by another booth. As soon as I looked up, there was a girl from my old neighborhood. We greeted one another as I introduced my husband.

Starting to relax just a little, my husband turned to me and asked, "How do you know that we won't be hurt or something." I simply replied, "The people know how to celebrate by honoring their city, and they are proud of it. Not everyone is bad, and not everything is bad. Everyone including criminals take a break to celebrate their city once in a while. I told you to trust me." And so the day rolled on as dusk was approaching. My husband asks, "Where is the car show?" I simply replied, "Well darling, they roll them out of these parts before dark usually, but I could be wrong." So we never saw a car show, but we celebrated with the people and had a wonderful and enjoyable day. I think it was the first time I ever saw my husband so quiet. I just led the way through the crowds and the Taste of East Chicago while watching the joyful people dance away. It felt good to be back in the area, and now my husband knew what part of the country I was from with firsthand experience. It was a wonderful and adventurous trip. I guess I still needed to work on my map skills, but who needs maps anyways, right?

## Chapter 53 The glasses

While taking a break in writing this book, I stopped to make dinner and dropped one of the spices all over the floor. My husband walked by smiling and reminded me what a klutz I am. I have to tell you a little something about myself. I totally break everything. At least once a week kind of thing. I guess it's just me. I do have dry spells where I don't break something for a while, but that is less common. He adores me most of the time, but sometimes he has to fix it. We had this key bowl where we kept the car keys way up in the china cabinet. He walked me into the kitchen one day and showed me where he put a pair of special eyeglass. I was told not to touch these glasses because they had special features to make things appear larger or smaller, like a magnifying glass. They were a little pricey, so he made sure to put them up somewhere they wouldn't get broken. He placed them next to the key bowl in the cabinet and told me no matter what to not touch them. Really? Why would I do that? Especially after he told me not to. I had no use for them. I reassured him that I would not touch them. Then of course true to my nature, you guessed it, I had a little accident. While reaching in for my keys in the bowl, my coat sleeve caught the corner of his glasses as they fell on the floor. I picked up his unique glasses to put them back, but they were broken. Now what? I broke the glasses! I didn't want to tell him, especially after I promised I wouldn't touch them. I had already broken two other things that week. I inventively got the super glue out of the drawer and tried to fix them myself. I didn't think I did too badly of a job with my glue work.

After fixing them, I gently put the glasses back in the cabinet and left for the day. A couple of days later, he went to get his glasses out of the cabinet to use them. All I heard was,"Get in here right now!" I didn't know what the excitement was all about as I made my way quickly to the kitchen. He had his glasses in his hand, and like a parent scolding a child he asked, "Did you break my glasses? Didn't I tell you? Didn't I tell you specifically not to touch my glasses?" I bashfully said with my head down while sweeping my foot back and forth, "Yes, I guess I did break them, but it was really an accident." He said, "The knobs won't turn on the side, and there is super glue on it! Did you try to fix them?" I replied quietly while nodding my head up and down, "Uh huh." Then with a huge smile, he started to laugh and began to tell me what a terrible job I did trying to fix them. He showed me how bad my work was with the super glue still smeared on the side. We both laughed until we almost cried. It was absolutely hysterical. He always forgave me for breaking stuff. At the same time, he also found it to be just part of my adorable cuteness, as he puts it, and always found it hard to be mad at me. He nicknamed me My Little Adorable. I asked him, "Why do you love me so much?" He simply replied, "Because you are just so adorable. You are just too cute."

## Chapter 54 The separation

Now somewhere in this book it was mentioned that my husband had an accent back when my family first met him at a Christmas gathering. He came from Europe. Like many immigrants, he arrived in America for a better life. I guess being in the career I had been in, I was used to clients with plenty of accents and his obvious accent really didn't stand out to me. I just loved him for who he was and he loved me. I looked at it as the same reason my family from Europe many generations back immigrated to America to make a better life, too. Also the fact of living in Europe myself, I got a glimpse of the downside of that world while living there and having my daughter being born overseas. I had plenty of ties to it. When I met my husband, he was already in America. I wasn't part of his plan, nor was he part of mine. Ultimately as both of our first marriages ended, our lives together began. I was thrust into the world of immigration. It took ten grueling years to go through the immigration process. Unfortunately, he had to go back to Europe without me while dealing with a family emergency as we continued our immigration process. Our families were oceans apart, and we had to completely trust one another. That was not part of the plan with him leaving. However, I was always grateful for the short separation as he got to be with his ill mother one last time before she passed away peacefully later on. Upon his return, we accomplished getting his full citizenship together with determination and hard work. Immigration was a very tedious process, long and complicated.

To me it was well worth it, and it was the greatest gift I could ever be a part of. It was just another example of our undeniable bond. Soon, I would find out he would give me an even greater gift of love in return.

## Chapter 55 He never let me fall

After returning and being reunited, I had to have abdominal surgery. It was supposed to be a simple procedure and low risk. Anything and everything went wrong, and an infection set in. I had to be opened up again and left wide open while having wound care for 6 months full of infection. With my stomach cut wide opened from hip to hip, my husband delicately twice a day would care for me. Bandage after bandage. Month after month. My husband was worn out, both mentally and physically from not knowing if I was really going to live or die. Death was at my door, and it was very serious. I had gray fluids pouring out of my gaping wound across my entire stomach, and I was very, very ill. As wonderful of a caregiver that he was to me, he would make sure all of my dressings were packed in my stomach so I could be with my children. He knew how much that meant to me. Defiant and no matter how bad I felt, I would detach myself from this pump I had to use to spend time with my children. Wherever I was, a ballgame or school event, I would secretly re-attach myself to the small pump to keep the infection drawn out of my body. Only my husband and close family members knew. All the while, I was still defending myself as a mother. I hid the stomach tubes for my medical pump under my jacket so my children wouldn't see them and become afraid for me, and they never knew. Without wavering, he loved me and cared for me with loving eyes every day.

I have to say that if it wasn't for him, I know I would not be here today. That is a big part of why I wrote this very book.

I especially want people to know what it is really like being loved by someone unconditionally. Until you are faced with adversities, that very love comes through. This man's true love is what kept me alive. Every morning and each night he triaged my open wound day after day until it finally closed, and I pulled through. The scar on my stomach is an everyday reminder of the love that my husband has for me. I proudly see it as a symbol of his love, and not an old ugly scar. He always looks at my scar passionately as our triumph together, and we celebrate it as a milestone in our relationship.

Two years later, I began to have strange symptoms. My hair was falling out more than usual and my bones ached very badly. It was just strange. Finally after much testing, I had a CT scan done on my brain. It was there that they found it. With my husband valiantly by my side, I was told I had a brain tumor. I had a tumor sitting behind my eyes. As explained to me, it would be something I could live a long life with. Also explained to me was the worst case scenario that I could die from its complications. One of the biggest complications I faced was losing my eye sight. My two younger children were still in school, and I kept this diagnosis from all of them. I did not want them to worry until I felt that each one of my children was old enough to understand and handle the news. To this day as I am writing this book, I still have the tumor and it is monitored for growth. I have regular checks on my eyes and retinas to make sure the tumor hasn't grown. If the tumor presses on the retinas, it can cause double vision. I may become legally blind.

I had to stop writing this book for a little bit to go to my eye doctor to have my tumor checked again and have photos of my retinas taken. I don't think about it every day. The tumor is just there. What good would that do? You should know me better than that by now. So far, so good.

I guess you can say surgeries for me definitely never go as planned. Playing sports over the years and getting a bit older, my knees were failing. After my last son's high school graduation, the decision was made by my physician that I had to have knee surgery. The first knee went without any problem. The second surgery, not so well. As life never goes as planned, my second knee continued to have complications. After I had a third surgery and almost 240 stitches later in all, complications from the anesthesia had temporarily paralyzed my leg. Not realizing I was paralyzed, I went to stand up for the first time. Without having any feeling, I tried to stand up with two nurses helping me. From the paralysis I couldn't do it, and we all began to fall on the slippery floor. As I remember it clearly, my husband was in the distant corner of the room and miraculously reached his body and stretched beyond belief from across the room to catch me. His extraordinary effort prevented me from falling, and he turned to me and said while holding me up, "I never let you fall." After I had the third surgery, I was set in a traction machine for weeks. I already fended off infection from the beginning, but I got worse. I had to have an I V attached to a port in my arm to pump tons of antibiotics into my body. After being released from the hospital, a travel nurse was sent to the house to give my husband training on how to change my fluids twice a day. He would get up at 2 am every morning before going to work, and he would change out the antibiotics. Then he would come home from work and do the same thing. Week after week, he lovingly and tenderly changed my antibiotics out. No matter how tired he was, I was always his first priority. With his loving support and dedication, I graduated from a walker to crutches, to a cane, then to no cane at all. With his unwavering dedication, I got better and learned how to walk again with his love every step of the way. If it hurt, he kissed my leg. If I couldn't walk, he picked me up and we walked together. If I could not go anymore, he encouraged me to keep going.

With his love, I got to walk alone again for the first time. I owe him so much for giving me the ability to walk again.

## Chapter 56 It's hard to get anything done

My husband and I are absolutely so ridiculously in love. Each day he keeps working with me on my strengthening and walking. As a treat, he pampers me with a pedicure and always puts my shoes on for me at the beauty shop. I get gazes from the ladies, and one once told me how jealous she was of me. I simply reply with a smile, and turn to him with another smile. Never in my wildest dreams would I have ever guessed there was such a great man that loved me so much. We always promised one another as he put it, "I will never break your heart, and I simply reply…"And I won't break yours either, my darling."

Since the beginning, I am showered with flowers for no reason at all. He surprises me sometimes with a small gift or something practical to use. It's not unusual for me to find a little something at my desk he wanted me to have. In return, I make him his favorite dinners or leave him out his favorite candy. Believe it or not, I love to fold his laundry and even match his socks! It is hard at times to get anything done in the house because we are so inseparable, but we both agreed to separate from time to time get any individual projects done. Saying I love you throughout the day isn't unusual. We will call out to one another from another room just to remind each other. He always makes sure to find my favorite shows or the program Shark Week on the television for me. He usually can get a little something done while I am immersed in shark adventures.

He is just so good to me. I don't really know why he is so good to me all the time, but I can say that he is just a wonderful man. He is the one thing in my life that I never expected, and I am one hell of a fortunate woman.

## Chapter 57 Make it Simple

We bought a little house together, now that the kids are grown. We are still young enough to enjoy a long future together, at least that's the plan. The house is just right for our needs. It was a fixer upper in the neighborhood with all of its walls colored in bright red, canary yellow, hunter green, plum purple, and Georgia peach. It needed some TLC, that's for sure. I found the house. My husband was not totally convinced it could look like anything special, but I was an artist. I had a vision of what it could look like. I promised him we could make it look spectacular again. We completed each room together with new paint with our favorite colors. With his ingenuity, we enclosed the back patio. Our covered porch has a swing on it to watch outside and enjoy the evenings by candlelight if we want to. The dining room was hunter green, and we painted it with really nice grays and blacks with white trim. I thought one dining wall would look nice with some matching wooden planks on it. My husband had a better idea. We would wallpaper it with gray and black panel designs on it. NO!! Not more wallpaper! Eventually we compromised, and this time it was a lot more fun wallpapering than when I was a little girl. This time, he held the wallpaper in place while I looked at our work. Then when it was done, we both backed up and looked at our own creation together arm in arm. It really turned out just right. Our bedroom is even painted like the colors of the blue waters with tranquil beach paintings. We always have given each other our own space, so he gets the basement and garage. It's not a fancy house, but it is ours. Just simple. It is a combination of both of our ideas of what we both like. I have to say living in a simple home is much cozier than any home out there. He calls it our Mini Mansion. If the walls could talk, they would tell you a lot of loving stories with tons of laughter. My husband is restoring an old T Bird with his garage. Someday when it is finished, I can't wait to ride around together in it.

# Chapter 58 Encouragement and the scrapbook

Apart from my dad, my husband is the one that encourages my artwork. He supplies me with paint and an easel to pursue my other passion besides cars. As I am writing this book, my dining room is filled with some paintings. I am restoring a painting for Mom that portraits the shores of Chicago sitting on the water. Actually, my special one I am painting is for my husband. It's not quite finished yet, but I hope he likes it when I am done. It is meant to represent a combination of both of our passions and our worlds coming together. The canvas will be filled with his favorite car, my horses, and our adventures together. He has inspired my work and reignited my passion to paint again after all these years from Oxford.

I always collected things over the years to put in a scrap book. My husband never knew what a scrap book was. As I explained to him, one day we need to look back at events or trips we took together in our lifetime. I came across an old business card. I am not even sure why I still had it. It was from the gypsy lady in New Orleans on Bourbon Street. Then I remembered what she said. She was right on some things. Funny, I even tried to call the number on her business card, but it was disconnected. I hoped she would have originally told me that I might win the lottery so I didn't have to work anymore and could become a world traveler. Honestly, she told me more than I ever knew that was to come in my life.

My husband and I put it safely back in the scrapbook and keep it there with the rest of our adventurous trips to car shows, car races, and Lake Michigan. He looked at me and said, "You and I will never win the lottery. You and I meeting was the lottery in life, you see?"

## My Final Chapter…At the end of the day

They tore down my old school in Gary. The memories on the shores still linger in the sands and dunes. Air shows from the Gary airport over Lake Michigan bring old friends back together these days. The community gatherings on the beach with fishing are still going on today bringing a sense of friendship and kindness with plenty of laughter.

I would love to report to you that today my children and I are very close, despite efforts to separate us. Not just separate me from my children, but my children from their mother. They have become responsible adults. My daughter learned a trade along the way and even put in new cabinets and faucets for my mom. She even fixes her own car sometimes. She has a beautiful soul, but with a little silliness and sass like her mother. My oldest son is in the IT field, and is married to a beautiful bi-lingual Spanish teacher. His wife is a kind and delightful person, and I just love having her as part of the family. He is an outstanding husband to her and a hard working provider. I am proud of the husband he has become more than he will ever know. My middle son became a successful Realtor with strong leadership and drive. He took a leap of faith to make a successful business for himself. He is self-made with a very strong drive for success. My youngest son got licensed in the finance world. He is also pursuing the real estate business alongside his brother and has natural salesmanship and charm. His determination and dedication will bring him far. He is really focused on being at the top with the world having no limits.

Yes, you can say I am a very proud momma of all of my children with our photo of all us together on my desk. Holiday gatherings at our house are joyful and plentiful, that's for sure. All of my children have the big hearts with a great sense of humor. It's not unusual to get a text from one of them with a good shark story or something else funny for me to enjoy. Sometimes we text back and forth just saying I love you and good night. Any chance we get, we spend time together. They turned out to be wonderful adults, but they were just as wonderful as children.

I have been told by my children that I am an inspiration to them, but truly they have been my inspiration. My two younger sons say they want to take care of me so I don't have to work anymore. They plan to be successful enough to buy me a condo of my choice on the water one day, and I would never have to work again. Maybe someday I will let them do that. In the mean time, I am in great hands..............

I have a message to my children. I love you, kids. Thank you for all the joy you bring to me every day by being your momma. Thank you for loving me so much in return. I couldn't ask for better children than you, and I am so glad you are mine. You will be loved until my last breath.

*My final words to you all...*

By the time you have read my candid memoir, you have probably laughed with me, wept with me, and maybe even raised an eyebrow or even two, but hopefully you also learned something from me. Thank you for being along with me through my journey in writing my book. I wanted to write this memoir to be an inspiration to all of you reading it that has had heartache or disappointment in your life. I am here today to say that life is what it is, ultimately good and bad. You only get one life, one. If everything in life was always good, your strength could never be tested to show how truly strong you can be. Let the good and bad and the joys in your journey become the outline of your own chapters in life. Let the scars in your life be your story and wear them proudly. Make peace with the past and thank those who have wronged you, even if you still don't like who they are. Let life test you. Always be true to yourself and keep laughter close by. When you meet the person of your dreams, don't hold back. It only happens once in a lifetime. Just go for it! Look at life as an adventure and learn from it. Throw away the maps, and let life take you to places you've never been before. If I die tomorrow, I know that I will die as an extremely loving mom and a truly loving wife and will be remembered very fondly. If I live tomorrow, I live each and every moment full of happiness and no regrets...My children tell me how strong I am, but they are part of the reason I am that way. They are my true warriors. I tell them to take what I have taught them and use it positively in their life. Just keep going! And remember that all the good and bad in life defines who were truly are. The life scars we carry are a reminder to never ever give up and keep moving forward...

I know my children will always be ok if I am not around one day, but I won't be far. That is my promise. I love them so much, but you already know that.

And very importantly, to the man who never let me fall, my dearest husband. It has been best time in my life being your wife, and an honor to have you at my side. You are my bestie. Thank you for all the support a man can ever give, and thank you for the undeniable love you show me every day by loving me for who I am. There will never be a man on this earth made of flesh and blood like you. You loved me when I was successful, and you loved me when I had lost everything. You loved me when I was sick, and you loved me when I was well. You loved me even when I accidentally broke some of your stuff, and still loved me when I even tried to fix them. With all of my silliness and clumsiness, you still adored me. Thank you for being my legs when I couldn't walk. Thank you for healing and packing my wounds when I couldn't. Thank you for saving my life when I came so close to losing it. Thank you for making me smile when I needed a good laugh. Thank you for holding my hand on our very first date. Thank you for celebrating with me when I came home with good news, and holding me when it was not. Thank you for being so strong for me when I needed your strength. Thank you for selflessly fighting many battles with me and for me. My darling, thank you so much for giving me your loving support to write this book. I love you from the deepest part of my soul. You really did win my heart from the second I saw you for the first time and fell in love with you...............

*At the end of the day, my life has been a true adventure, and I have no regrets...*